TO MY PARENTS,
Howard and Virginia Bryant,
who have covered my
life with a concert
of prayer since the
day we entered
the Kingdom together.

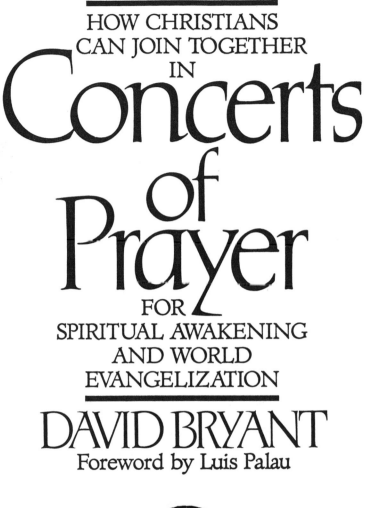

HOW CHRISTIANS
CAN JOIN TOGETHER
IN

Concerts
of
Prayer

FOR
SPIRITUAL AWAKENING
AND WORLD
EVANGELIZATION

DAVID BRYANT
Foreword by Luis Palau

GL
Regal Books
A Division of GL Publications
Ventura, California, U.S.A.

Published by Regal Books
A Division of Gospel Light
Ventura, California, U.S.A.
Printed in U.S.A.

Regal Books is a ministry of Gospel Light, an evangelical Christian publisher dedicated to serving the local church. We believe God's vision for Gospel Light is to provide church leaders with biblical, user-friendly materials that will help them evangelize, disciple and minister to children, youth and families.

It is our prayer that this Regal Book will help you discover biblical truth for your own life and help you meet the needs of others. May God richly bless you.

For a free catalog of resources from Regal Books/Gospel Light please contact your Christian supplier or call 1-800-4-GOSPEL.

Scripture quotations in this publication are from:
The HOLY BIBLE: NEW INTERNATIONAL VERSION. Copyright © 1973, 1978, 1984 by the International Bible Society. Used by permission of Zondervan Bible Publishers.

Library of Congress Cataloging in Publication Data

Bryant, David, 1945—
      Concerts of prayer.

      Bibliography. p.
      1. Prayer. 2. Spiritual life. I. Title.
BV210.2.B77   1984   248.3'2
ISBN 0-8307-1301-8   84-17916

Grateful appreciation is expressed to all those who granted permission to include their copyrighted material:
      In chapter 5, Dr. Richard Halverson is quoted from *Between Peril and Promise* by James R. and Elizabeth Newby. Used by permission of Thomas Nelson Publishers.
Any omission of credits or permissions granted is unintentional. The publisher requests documentation for future printings.

4 5 6 7 8 9 10 11 12 13 / 02 01 00 99 98 97 96

Rights for publishing this book in other languages are contracted by Gospel Literature International (GLINT). GLINT also provides technical help for the adaptation, translation, and publishing of Bible study resources and books in scores of languages worldwide. For further information, contact GLINT, Post Office Box 4060, Ontario, California, 91761-1003, U.S.A., or the publisher.

CONTENTS

Foreword, Luis Palau   9
Acknowledgments   11
Introduction:
Concerts of Prayer: What Are They?   13

Part I: THE PRIORITY OF A MOVEMENT OF   15
         PRAYER FOR THE WORLD

  1. Ordinary People at the Threshold   17
     A Tale for Ordinary People
     Seismologists Testing for the Extraordinary
     "Readings" of My Own

  2. Concerted Prayer: 25
     The Frontline in World Evangelization
     The Force of Concerted Prayer
     Frontline Priorities of Concerted Prayer
     Distinctives of a Concert of Prayer
     The Force of Concerted Prayer Is with Us

  3. Anatomy of a Movement of Prayer   31
     Zechariah 8: A Look at the Context
     Zechariah's Prayer Vision
     "Let Us Go at Once!"

  4. Beyond the Threshold: 39
     The Hope Toward Which We Pray
     Spiritual Awakening: What Is It? Who Needs It?
     When the Father Wakes Us Up
     To See Christ's Fullness in New Ways
     To Trust, Love and Obey Him in New Ways
     To Move with Him in the Fulfillment of His Global Cause
     So That . . . Together
     Conclusion: Gandhi and Awakening

5. **Spiritual Awakening:**
   Four Good Reasons to Look for It!   51
   Reason 1—The Divine Pattern
   Reason 2—The Dark Prospects
   Reason 3—Our Disturbing Paralysis
   Reason 4—The Dramatic Preparations

6. **Pacesetters:**
   Leading the Way to the Threshold   69
   Secret Service Agents
   The Costs
   Will You Be One?

Part II: STEPS TOWARD A MOVEMENT OF   75
        PRAYER FOR THE WORLD

7. **Three Steps to Get Us Started**   77
   Repentance: Making Room for Spiritual Awakening
   Unity: Providing Wineskins for Spiritual Awakening
   Daily Disciplines: Getting in Shape for Spiritual Awakening

8. **Mobilizing a Movement of Prayer:**   87
   You Can Do It!
   Problems with Prayer
   Principles for Mobilization
   Use of a Covenant
   Possible Pitfalls
   A Consultation on Concerts of Prayer
   Forming a Steering Committee

9. **Organizing a Concert of Prayer:**   95
   Of Course You Can!
   Variety Is the Spice . . .
   A Suggested Format
   More Guidelines

10. **Agenda for Concerted Prayer:**   115
   Shape of Prayers to Come
   Get It Growing
   Issues for Prayer

11. **Hey, Leader, Strike Up the Band:**   129
   Marching Out in a Concert of Prayer
   The Three Paces of Intercession
   Solidarity: Agreeing with God
   Advocacy: Standing up for Others
   Pursuit: Pressing on for a Change

Postscript:
Try the Next Seven Years, for a Start!   137

Pacesetters Small Group Study Guide   139

Agenda for Consultation on Concerts of Prayer   151

Working Proposals for Consultation   154

A Call to Prayer—
1984 International Prayer Assembly   157

Notes   161

Video Training with the Author   163

ACKNOWLEDGMENTS

I've had the undeserved privilege to work for over eight years within the expanding ministry of InterVarsity Christian Fellowship. I want to thank President James McLeish and many staff and students for their creative efforts to grapple with and implement the ideas in this book. It has resulted in deeper, sharper thinking on my part.

I acknowledge a special debt to John Kyle, IVCF missions director, who has been mentor, guide, father and friend—all in one—over these years. Graciously God allowed us to find in each other reflections of common dreams and visions that will not be silent.

I'm also indebted to friends on the National Prayer Committee and the Lausanne Intercession Advisory Group, and to thousands in churches who've responded to my Concert of Prayer Seminars. They have provided vital input into this book both by suggestions and faithful examples.

To my secretary, Joy Mykytiuk, as well as Kathy Dobbins, Neil Bartlett and all my colleagues at InterVarsity Missions, my deepest thanks for hard labor and encouraging prayers. The same goes for Bill Greig and my friends at Regal Books.

Finally, to Robyne I can only say: "You *still* walk with me as one . . . in the gap. But even more so, now that we've been walking shoulder-to-shoulder with concerts of prayer. I couldn't imagine taking these steps without you."

FOREWORD

David Bryant's book is a masterpiece. I plan to use it heavily, to recommend it widely and, God willing, to give away scores of copies.

This book has a sense of anointing from God. It draws from history to make powerful points about revival, world evangelism and the missionary thrust of the Church.

I believe that this book could be used of God to stir revival in thousands of lives. I truly believe it is a book that God could use to lift up an army of young people from this generation to evangelize our world. It is biblical, deeply spiritual and intensely practical. Quite a combination!

I hope this book spreads across America and around the world in English and in translated form.

—Luis Palau
Portland, Oregon

INTRODUCTION
Concerts of Prayer:
What Are They?

As Christians we experience prayer on many meaningful levels: through personal devotions, in small Bible study groups, at Sunday school, before meals, during worship. But the level of concerted prayer envisioned here differs from the rest (though every level of prayer is richly enhanced by it). That is why we give it the distinguishing name "concerts of prayer."

In the 1740s, Puritan divine Jonathan Edwards defined "concerts of prayer" in the very title of a book he circulated to equip Christians then for the prayer movement that undergirded what historians often call The First Great Awakening. The title? *An Humble Attempt to Promote Explicit Agreement and Visible Union of God's People in Extraordinary Prayer of the Revival of Religion and the Advancement of Christ's Kingdom on Earth.* Concerts of prayer, as defined by Edwards in this title, can be found throughout Scripture. For example: 2 Chronicles 15:1-15; Zechariah 8:18-23; Acts 4:23-31; Revelation 5:7-10 (see also 8:3-4). In his book, Edwards borrowed the vision of Zechariah 8 to paint a vivid picture of prayer concerts. Zechariah describes the attitude, the agenda, the impact and the means for mobilizing such a prayer movement. His vision has been realized repeatedly throughout church history and in prayer movements emerging across North America right now as well as in the global Church.

What makes concerts of prayer so different? For one thing, the *makeup* consists of a broader representation of the pray-ers. Christians unite across various boundaries: denominational, institutional, ministry, social, generational and even (minor) doctrinal ones. They meet around larger biblical concerns for spiritual awakening and world evangelization.

Accordingly, the *focus* in prayer concerts is quite specific: the *agenda* is limited to issues that fall under two main sweeps in Scripture: (1) prayer for God to reveal to His Church the *fullness* of Christ as Lord in her midst (revival, renewal, awakening) and (2) prayer for the resulting *fulfillment* of His global cause through His Church among all the nations, including their own (missions, world evangelization, advancement of the Kingdom).

Also the *dynamics* in prayer concerts are often unique. "Concert" (from the same root as "concerned") means that people are united in sustained commitment to the Lord, to one another and to the answers they seek until God grants "fullness" and "fulfillment". Also, concerts of prayer, like musical concerts, involve the dynamics of a harmonious celebration—like a grand symphony—as pray-ers blend their hearts, minds and voices by faith in God's Word. Rejoicing, repenting and making requests, they intercede in harmony with all God has promised for His Church and for His world. They submit to the Holy Spirit who orchestrates each player meeting so that one prayer-theme builds on another according to the will of God. The whole climaxes in a composition of intercession in Jesus' name which the Father delights both to hear and to answer abundantly.

PART I
THE PRIORITY OF A MOVEMENT OF PRAYER FOR THE WORLD

1
ORDINARY PEOPLE AT THE THRESHOLD

We *ordinary people* cannot fit our lives into pre-formed, Styrofoam boxes. We cannot manage life as well as we would like, at least not in our secret places. We cannot get all the strings tied; it won't wrap up the way we want it. For us, survival is often the biggest success story we dare hope for.

Ordinary people feel too tired a lot. They come to church and listen to words about a grace that has made life all right at the core. But they are often so muzzled by self-pity, so shackled by anger, and so paralyzed by their own real hurts that they cannot find the extra reserve of power to open their hearts to the reality of Jesus Christ and the fact of his grace. God needs to open the door.

The surprise is that God does give us the gift. Sometimes. And sometimes we accept it.[1]

I must confess, Lewis Smedes, who wrote these words, has *me* figured out pretty well. I am an ordinary person! How about you? From God's perspective, of course, anyone created and redeemed by Him can hardly be called "ordinary." Yet, in our day-to-day routine we often feel very ordinary, don't we?

But Smedes also puts his finger on the other, often extraordinary, dimension of who we are. He calls our attention to the unusual, the surprising, the miraculous ways God invades our lives. Listen as he goes on!

> Sometimes people are sure that everything is all wrong and they are tired of trying to make it right. *Then God comes* quietly to tell them that he is around them, above them, under them, in them, and ahead of them, and that with this surrounding shield of strong love, they are going to be all right.
>
> Sometimes people are in the grip of anger that chokes their hearts, stifles their joy, and smothers every intimate relationship. *Then God comes* in to break the chain of anger and liberate an ordinary person for a new try at love.
>
> Sometimes people live in quiet terror of their own death. *Then God comes* in to give them a reason for being very glad to be alive just for today.
>
> Sometimes people brood over a depressing memory of some rotten thing they did and cannot forget or forgive themselves for. *Then God comes* in to open their hearts to receive the gifts of other ordinary people's forgiveness and so come to forgive themselves.
>
> Sometimes ordinary people wrap themselves like mummies in the suffocating sackcloth of their own self-hatred; and God comes to open their eyes to the extraordinary wonder of their great worth.[2]

Many Christian leaders today believe that God is preparing to do what Smedes describes but on a broader, more intense, more earth-shaking scale than any of us have ever known. A whole host of ordinary people are currently poised at the threshold of an extraordinary work of God in the life of His whole Church. And the world is waiting!

A TALE FOR ORDINARY PEOPLE
On the visual display of my mental terminal occurs a repeat-

ing drama—a vision of sorts as vivid as if it actually happened a moment ago. I see myself standing at the far end of a darkened hallway lined with many doors. All are shut and locked, but one. Light penetrates the hallway through a partially opened door at the far end. Curious, I want to find out more.

Gradually, I walk down the hallway toward the light. The closer I get to the door, the more brilliant and delightful the light appears to be. I even begin to feel its warmth. It almost dances.

But when I reach the threshold I find neither courage nor freedom to fling the door open and burst into the radiant room beyond. Awe and fear mingle with anticipation. I hesitate to knock, yet I know if I do, an invitation to enter eventually will come.

I knock deliberately and boldly, compelled by the conviction that until there is an answer I have little else to live for, as the hallway behind me promises little worth seeking.

My video-vision continues; I'm knocking more rapidly now. Gradually I realize I am not alone. Others are quietly rising out of the shadows of the hallway to join me. We knock together now, harder and harder, almost in a frenzy! Our knocking attracts still others, until the threshold is crowded with determined people from the shadows who, having seen something of the light, desire to step inside, into the full radiance of it.

My eyes glance for a moment back down the hallway. Suddenly my heart leaps! It strikes me that when the door finally does swing open to us and we are able to move into the glorious treasures that lie beyond, the blessing will not be for us alone. The light into which we step will, at the same moment, pour beyond us to the far ends of the hallway, dispelling any dimness that remains. And how many of those locked doors will those dazzling rays pierce, penetrating the rooms like a laser, driving out of them the even greater darkness there and calling many from the icy shadows of death.

What does it all mean? From the first moment I recorded these pictures, the interpretation was obvious. The knocking on the door is prayer. The light coming through the crack in the door is the "light of the knowledge of the glory of God in the face of Christ" (2 Cor. 4:6). The hallway represents the Church today, much of which survives in the twilight zone of all that God originally intended for us, in us, and through us. The sealed side-rooms symbolize enclaves and even whole nations, where Christ is not known.

The locked doors, waiting to be overcome by grace and truth, include structures and powers, injustices and crises, cultures and languages, persuasions old and new, that raise formidable barriers against the advancement of the Kingdom.

Those who gather at the threshold with me are members of the Lord's company—ordinary people who, already drawn to the light and benefiting from it, are hungry to know the fullness of Christ in their lives and to see the fulfillment of His purposes among the nations. The flinging wide of the central door is "spiritual awakening." It is not so much our taking more of Christ into the Church as it is Christ inviting us into more of Himself and His Kingdom. But once the door is fully open, it releases more of the intense light of the gospel and its power into the Church and thus among all peoples.

The chorus of knockers represents the current development of concerted prayer for spiritual awakening. It also describes the critical dimension of such a movement where those who are determined are seeking to enter wholly and obediently in His light gather others to join in the search. They're unwilling to stop knocking until God swings open the door into the brilliant immensity of Christ's global cause. In fact, the door on which we knock is Jesus Christ Himself ("whatever you ask in *my* name"); He is the end of our search, He is also the way in.

What a strategic place for "ordinary people" to be—standing on the threshold of a new work of God in all our lives and throughout the earth. You see, this drama goes far beyond expanding individual spiritual experiences. It's possible for a whole generation of God's praying people to be surprised (Smede's word) by Him.

SEISMOLOGISTS TESTING FOR THE EXTRAORDINARY

Once we gather at the threshold, however, our initial experience may feel more like being caught in the middle. There's enough darkness in the hallway that we don't want to go back, and there's such promising light before us that we only want to go forward. But we can't move beyond the door that's ajar until *God* takes us on together. That's where the Church seems to be right now. We can neither go backward or forward, so we must go down corporately—on our knees—in prayer, at the threshold of God's new work in our midst. And there we must wait in hope for something to break loose.

In a parallel way, many social analysts recognize that the world at large is united in a mood of wonder and fearful transition between eras, a time of parenthesis. Though some call this a moment of fashionable pessimism, when we're weary with the past but disenchanted about the future, John Naisbitt, in his best-seller *Megatrends,* disagrees. Ours is really a time full of promise, he writes, when the world senses itself to be on the threshold of earthshaking possibilities:

> Although the time between eras is uncertain, it is a great and yeasty time, filled with opportunity. If we can learn to make uncertainty our friend, we can achieve much more than in stable eras.
>
> In stable eras, everything has a name and everything knows its place, and we can leverage very little.
>
> But in the time of the parenthesis we have extraordinary leverage and influence—individually, professionally, and institutionally—if we can only get a clear sense, a clear conception, a clear vision, of the road ahead.[3]

If this is how secularists feel about our historic moment, we Christians-in-transition should be no less hopeful, but have a far greater vision of where things are headed and, even more, who is really in charge. For the threats of serious national and international upheaval—not to mention technological revolution—should never negate our anticipating a God-given era of glorious upheaval in the Church that will have national and international repercussions for Christ's Kingdom. We ordinary people need to hear this now more than ever.

In fact, we may be at the threshold of a spiritual awakening qualitatively different from any previous one. With a mature foundation laid in knowledge of Scripture, in understanding the ministry of the Holy Spirit, in commitments to Body unity, in the initiative of the laity, and in its ready heart for total world evangelization, the Church today may be more equipped for revival than in any other era.

"READINGS" OF MY OWN

In my 21 years as a Christian, I too have become a seismologist. Though I still feel like an amateur, I sense the rightness of others' predictions. Let me describe some "readings" from my personal seismograph.

When I was a pastor I quickly realized that without a deep work of God, both in individuals and in the corporate life of our church, there would be neither the environment nor the sustaining foundation for fostering committed Christians. That's when God first helped me understand the essentiality of spiritual awakening and its prelude, concerted prayer.

As a pastor in Kent, Ohio in 1970, I was forced to God's threshold after witnessing the Kent State University shootings that fateful day in May. The trauma of that tragic incident not only sealed the mood of our country about Vietnam but, ultimately, the course of history and nations.

Our church, as a body, felt convicted. The impact we were having on the world for Christ was negligible compared to the impact of the student-national guard confrontation on the KSU campus. By fall, five men in the church joined me in seeking some answers from God. We agreed to meet for six weeks of prayer, four nights a week, two hours a night.

The first night we met, we sat there, staring at each other with half smiles as if to say, "Well, what do we do now?" None of us had ever prayed like this before. One suggested we pray through Scripture. That made sense. We chose Ephesians. And why not? Ephesians has six chapters and we were committed to meet for six weeks.

And what an unforgettable six weeks. You can't pray through Scripture like Ephesians and stay the same. Paul swept us along in God's purposes for the nations and the Church. And I believe we saw some key evidences of spiritual awakening as a result.

We grew, as a congregation, in a new appreciation for world evangelization and in a desire to begin giving ourselves to whatever God would ask of us in serving Christ's global cause. This was a new experience for me, and it could have been spawned only in prayer. Previously, I had run from missions, even in seminary. In thrilling ways, God has worked through that little church over the past 15 years to bring Christ to the nations.

CONCERTED PRAYER
The Frontline in World Evangelization

Not long ago I heard Scottish expositor Eric Alexander talk about the apostles' ministry priority in Acts 6:4,7. He said: "The frontline in world evangelization is the Word of God and prayer."

He's right. World evangelization demands many things of us, but we can never get any closer to advancing the gospel among the nations than to link our hearts around God's Word, turning its visions and promises into concerted prayer. Revelation 5 and 8 suggest the mingled prayers of God's people, ascending together like incense before His throne, bear directly on the out-working of both redemption (chap. 5) and justice (chap. 8) among the nations.

THE FORCE OF CONCERTED PRAYER

I can't fully explain *how* prayer changes things in world evangelization. It may be that prayer fits into the sovereignty of God in the same way that time lapse photography makes a rose open up before my eyes in 30 seconds. If the rose hadn't unfolded naturally over a previous period of two or three days, there would be nothing on film. Similarly, as God's people unite to seek all that He has determined to do, prayer, like the movie camera, accelerates and intensifies the unfolding of all God has already willed for His Kingdom. Prayer theologian O. Hallesby put it this way:

> When God changes the divine world-economy as a result of man's prayers, we mean that he governs the world with such a degree of elasticity that he can alter his methods as circumstances here below require, be they good or bad. He does not alter his kingdom plans, only the means and methods whereby he at each moment seeks to accomplish them.[1]

In other words, none of us is able to begin to untangle every crisis or meet every need in the world. But through prayer we can accelerate and intensify God's methods for extending His Kingdom among the nations. We can do more than watch history happen; through our prayers we *make* history together. Or, as my friend Dick Eastman observes, in prayer we "make room for God." After that, anything can happen!

So prayer is God's frontline way of getting things done. But it needs to be *united* prayer. How else can we explain that the Christian Church today is 83 million times larger than when it first began? How else do you explain that the outward advance of the gospel is the longest human endeavor in the history of mankind? How else do you explain that, directly or indirectly, the Scriptures have altered for good most major cultures on earth today? The outstanding answer is this: again and again, in one new generation of His people after another, God has raised up pacesetters in prayer who have united to seek His will on earth, and God has answered them far beyond what they asked or thought.

FRONTLINE PRIORITIES OF CONCERTED PRAYER

As I have studied these matters, key principles have emerged. Unlike Luther with his 95 theses, I have only *five* to offer! But I would be delighted to nail them on the bulletin board of any campus or church in this country and return a week later (as Luther did at Wittenburg University) to discuss the issues with lay people, pastors, missionaries, or students who would desire to do so. How would you respond to them?

1. World evangelization, its fruits and its fulfillment through

Christ's global Church, is from beginning to end the work of God (Col. 1:17-23).

2. Therefore, only He can awaken the Church to renewed zeal for Christ, His Kingdom, and His global cause, and create an environment that fosters Christians who are wholly dedicated to the task of world evangelization (Eph. 1:16-23).

3. The Church pursues God's work of awakening and world evangelization through united, concerted, sustained prayer, declaring our desire to see His glory revealed and acknowledging our utter dependence on Him to advance His Kingdom (Eph. 6:16-20).

4. Such a movement of united prayer focuses on the two major sweeps of Scripture: the *fullness* of Christ manifested in His Church (revival) for the advancement of His Kingdom, and the *fulfillment* of His global cause (evangelization) (Matt. 6:9-13).

5. Such a movement of united prayer is normally initiated by pioneers of faith who embrace God's redemptive purpose and set the pace for serving it through concerted prayer, encouraging many others thereby to follow (Acts 4:23-31).

DISTINCTIVES OF A CONCERT OF PRAYER

Concerted prayer is distinct from other prayer times in a number of ways. First, it's primarily a *movement* of prayer. It defines an effort to forge a coalition of praying people who regularly unite for a very specific agenda surrounding spiritual awakening and *world evangelization*. In concerts of prayer we work together toward consensus about all we want God to do within His Church and His World.

A concert of prayer requires a balanced concentration on two major sweeps: (1) fullness in the Body of Christ for (2) the fulfillment of His global cause. Both sweeps create healthy tension. A concert is designed to allow us to get at fullness and fulfillment in prayer as effectively as possible. This focus of concerted prayer rises from one common concern: zeal for God's glory. Prayer for fullness and fulfillment both seek God's glory among His people as well as among the unreached.

Often when I travel I find two kinds of prayer groups: (1) those who meet regularly to pray for renewal or revival in the

Church; (2) those who meet regularly to pray for local outreach, world missions or global crises. Rarely does the same person participate in both groups. Frequently, neither group is aware of the other yet the focus of the one should thrive on the other; the one should drive us to the other.

Prayer for the needs of the world urges us to pray for the Church to love Christ in such a way as to meet those needs (fullness). Seeking God's blessings for the Church, however, requires that we also pray for God to bring blessing and healing to the world through the Church (fulfillment). So you see, adding fulfillment issues to fullness prayers prevents a cop-out. Coupling fullness issues to fulfillment prayers prevents a burn-out. Put both together and we will leap out into all God has for us.

What would happen if both kinds of prayer groups would gather together sometimes? What if they shared their individual agendas, learning from one another how the two fit together? What if they blended into a great symphony of intercession that touched both prongs of God's Kingdom? Concerts of prayer provide a way to preserve the distinctive focus and commitment that is so critical for spiritual awakening which dawns as a combination of God's answers to fullness and fulfillment prayers in our time.

THE FORCE OF CONCERTED PRAYER IS WITH US

When Christians reach a point where they are convinced there are some things in the Church and in the world that God either cannot or will not do until they pray, then miracles begin to happen.

That's why the emergence of united prayer in the Church worldwide at this moment may be the first great miracle of the awakening just ahead, a sign of other miracles to come. When prayer is on the increase, then we can be sure revival is at hand.

No, I do not see swelling crowds gathering in concerted prayer—not yet. But the breadth of prayer efforts for revival across geographical, national, denominational, organizational and social lines, and the depth of the agenda surfacing in prayer groups everywhere, suggest very clearly that God is up to something extraordinary.

Over the past 10 years, the evangelical Church worldwide

has been united informally under the umbrella of the World Evangelical Fellowship (WEF) and the Lausanne Committee on World Evangelization (LCWE). WEF called 1983 "The Year of Prayer for Revival." LCWE's objectives for the 1980s and 1990s are: (1) to help organize Christians for a variety of cooperative efforts; (2) to promote spiritual renewal as the foundation for world evangelization; (3) to measure progress in order to focus on united prayer and other resources on the completion of the task of world evangelization. In the Lausanne occasional paper titled "Evangelism and Social Responsibility" this prayer strategy is spelled out clearly for us:

> We resolve ourselves, and call upon our churches, to take much more seriously the period of intercession in public worship; to think in terms of ten or fifteen minutes rather than five; to invite lay people to share in leading, since they often have deep insight into the world's needs; and to focus our prayers both on the evangelization of the world (closed lands, resistant peoples, missionaries, national churches, etc.) and on the quest for peace and justice in the world (places of tension and conflict, deliverance from the nuclear horror, rulers and governments, the poor and needy, etc.). We long to see every Christian congregation bowing down in humble and expectant faith before our Sovereign Lord.[2]

Here in our own country, God is giving the gift of prayer to the Church on a new scale. In Washington, D.C., an effort is underway to form prayer/think tanks where Christian leaders from all levels of society can gather in concerted prayer to seek God's wisdom on major national and international problems. This project, involving hundreds, walks hand-in-hand with monthly interdenominational concerts of prayer in the Washington area.

Also, in our nation's capital, an interdenominational body recently purchased Ralph Nader's old headquarters on Capitol Hill and has designated the building as the site of a 24-hour prayer watch for revival and world evangelization. Once a month those who use the building for prayer meet with others in a concert of prayer. Currently they are sending out teams around the nation to assist in the formation of a network of prayer concerts within—ultimately—all 50 state capitals.

In the student world, prayer ferment is also evident. The Campus Ministry director of InterVarsity Christian Fellowship recently called for renewal within our movement, suggesting that one of the clear evidences of renewal would be the reemergence of concerted prayer. And Operation Mobilization, as a part of their pre-field training for summer short-termers, conducts all-night "International Concerts of Prayer."

Campus Crusade for Christ has instituted a major thrust in united prayer. They've called on all their staff in the United States to set aside a half day a week to unite together in prayer. Looking at it as a businessman, Bill Bright told me that this effort was quite a stiff investment. Four hours a week times a 10,000-member staff at a minimum of $4 an hour equal millions of dollars a year invested in united prayer alone!

But, God has honored Crusade's resolve by giving them, in 1984, over 10,000 students actively participating in united prayer through the newly formed National Collegiate Prayer Alliance. The staff set the pace; their students caught the vision.

If prayer, praying people, and a movement of prayer are gifts of God, and if that movement of prayer is designed to mobilize God's people to do something about world evangelization, then this current breadth and depth of united prayer worldwide should encourage us all. And, if God is raising up a new surge of united prayer as a prelude to and foundation for all He is preparing to do among His people and to the ends of the earth, then all of God's praying people need to be in it together, and the sooner the better!

In light of the opportunities for the gospel all around us, is there any more strategic contribution any of us can make than to assist a movement of concerted prayer? And in light of the needs of the Church and the world, is there any alternative?

From a biblical perspective, what would we expect a contemporary concert of prayer movement to look like? That is the question we address in the next chapter.

3

THE ANATOMY OF A MOVEMENT OF PRAYER

In the divine economy, what should concerted prayer look like? How would God define its characteristics? By what principles does He want it to operate? These are important questions which must have biblical answers.

United prayer threads its way through Scripture from Israel in the land of bondage through a variety of episodes during the rule of the judges, the Levites serving in the Tabernacle, the exiles returning to rebuild the Temple, the people waiting eagerly before the Lord along the Jordan, and the prayer band that sent out Paul and Barnabas from Antioch.

But, more than any other, one Scripture passage has had a profound historical impact in the formation of prayer movements during the last 300 years. It's Zechariah's vision of concerted prayer (Zech. 8:18-23).

ZECHARIAH 8: A LOOK AT THE CONTEXT

Around 520 B.C., during the reign of Darius, king of Medo-Persia, Zechariah was sent by God to encourage the 42,000 exiles who, 16 years earlier, had returned to Jerusalem to rebuild the Temple. Although these exiles were only a remnant of the total Israelite population, they were people of faith and vision. Their mission was to rebuild the Temple to establish a witness to the world that God was in the midst of His people and was available to all who would seek Him. Their mission, if you will, was to rebuild a work of concerted prayer.

But 16 years had passed since their return, and they were discouraged. Not only did they find the task of rebuilding the Temple difficult but they were opposed by foreigners who had previously inhabited the land.

The same year, Zechariah went to Jerusalem, Haggai was also sent with a simple message from God: stop building your own houses (concentrating on your own needs and plans) and come together again to work on God's house. Only then, he told them, would they truly experience God's blessings in their personal lives. God promised that He would then accomplish a mission through them that would shake the heavens and the earth, causing the Temple to become the gathering place for all people. We read in Haggai that revival finally took place; God stirred up the spirits of leaders and citizens alike and they gave themselves to His priority: rebuilding the Temple to mobilize a movement of prayer among nations.

Then Zechariah and Haggai joined to help bring God's revival work to completion. Zechariah's message was one of prayer and awakening: "'Return to me, . . . and I will return to you,' says the Lord Almighty" (Zech. 1:3).

The book divides nicely into two major sections, with the vision for our study (Zech. 8:18-23) forming the climax of the first section, as it captures the mood and momentum of all that God revealed in the previous eight chapters.

ZECHARIAH'S PRAYER VISION

In chapter seven, Zechariah is faced with a confused delegation from Bethel. Though they are part of the faithful remnant, they fear that Zechariah's message of hope may be leading them away from a traditional time of mourning and fasting.

For 70 years, the Israelites had remembered the siege and destruction of Jerusalem by fasting four whole days. The fasts commemorated their defeat with a time of mourning over the disgrace of God's name before Gentiles, of remembering unfulfilled promises, and of asking themselves if there was any future for their nation at all. In the process, however, they undermined their hope that the spiritual poverty they had incurred in defeat would ever be fully removed. So they asked, "Should we not just continue our fasts, Zechariah, despite your promising visions?"

Zechariah's response goes right to the point. He tells them how God is still very jealous in His love for Zion. God intends to return to Zion and dwell there, and the city will become known as the City of Truth (not of disgrace). Zechariah tells them: "'It may seem marvelous to the remnant of this people at this time, but will it seem marvelous to me?' declares the Lord Almighty" (Zech. 8:6). Zechariah assures them that God determines to do good to them again, to fully revive them, and they need not be afraid.

Then he unveils the most strategic thing they should do next. He calls for unity within the remnant people as they speak truth to each other and render true and sound judgment in their courts, and love one another. But then he takes them further. He gives them a vision which is so certain that it is described as fact:

"Again the word of the Lord Almighty came to me. This is what the Lord Almighty says: 'The fasts of the fourth, fifth, seventh, and tenth months will become joyful and glad occasions and happy festivals for Judah. Therefore love truth and peace.'

"This is what the Lord Almighty says: 'Many peoples and the inhabitants of many cities will yet come, and the inhabitants of one city will go to another and say, "Let us go at once to entreat the Lord and seek the Lord Almighty. I myself am going." And many peoples and powerful nations will come to Jerusalem to seek the Lord Almighty and to entreat him.'

"This is what the Lord Almighty says: 'In those days ten men from all languages and nations will take firm hold of one Jew by the edge of his robe and say, "Let us go with you, because we have heard that God is with you"'" (Zech. 8:18-23).

In one sense, this vision gathers up and fulfills all the others that precede it (chap. 1-6); it also acts as a hinge to turn them toward God's restoring process, more vividly described in the remaining six chapters. God calls them in to prepare for concerted prayer for revival that would have international repercussions

Zechariah describes this prayer vision in terms of its hallmarks; God's anatomy of a movement of prayer. In another sense it is also an anatomy of spiritual awakening, for such a movement is evidence that God has already begun to revitalize their faith in Him. Let's examine four hallmarks of this anatomy: the attitude, agenda, impact, and ignition for concerts of prayer.

Hallmark: The Attitude

We hear a lot about prayer and fasting, but Zechariah calls for prayer and *feasting*! He tells the delegation from Bethel to stop fasting and start celebrating in anticipation of all the wonderful things God is preparing to do.

Their attitude was also to be marked with urgency. They were to "go at once," or as it reads in the Hebrew, "go going." This movement of prayer, set loose in dancing, was to be intense, determined, and persevering. Jonathan Edwards, the eighteenth century Puritan preacher, called the movement "extraordinary prayer." It is prayer that presses as far as it can go, even into the very Holy of Holies.

Two other words underscore the sense of urgency. "Entreat" means literally to travail as a woman travails in the final moments in giving birth, or as a person who is deathly sick might cry for help. Zechariah also tells us to "seek" the Lord, which more accurately means to search or strive after Him.

Both words suggest that prayer brings forth into the world something that is so precious and wonderful that all other concerns must be laid aside; that the agony of interceding for God's new work must become the primary focus of our efforts. It also means that, knowing how desperate and helpless we are apart from God's work on our behalf, we strive in prayer after the only One who can deliver us from our intolerable condition. In both cases, our prayers crackle with urgency. Certainly anticipation and urgency must mark our prayer lives, especially as we gather in concerted prayer for spiritual awakening.

Hallmark: The Agenda

And what is the objective of Zechariah's prayer movement? What are they praying about? What are they asking God to do?

In the Hebrew it says they are "seeking God," literally

"seeking the face of the Lord." On the surface, it might seem one could wrap up this prayer meeting in short order! Are we only to ask God to see His face? Is that all a concert of prayer is about?

Often the Hebrew words translated in English as "seek the Lord" or "God's presence" or "before the Lord" contain the key idea of seeking God's face. When you come right down to it, every prayer request you have ever made and every answer to prayer you have ever received is that God revealed His face. In fact, that is the bottom line of God's redeeming work throughout the ages: He's bringing the universe back before His face.

It was God's face that was turned toward Israel, as His great benediction on their wilderness mission toward the land of promise (Num. 6:22-27). The psalmist tells us that when God's face shines on His people, His salvation is made known before all the nations (Ps. 67). That's why Ezekiel was looking for someone to stand in the gap before God's face on behalf of a disobedient nation (Ezek. 22:30). Paul understood these truths well enough that when he describes the gospel treasure he was dispensing through his own apostolic ministry, he described it as the "light of the knowledge of the glory of God in the face of Christ" (2 Cor. 4:6). The book of Revelation carries us a step further, telling us that the greatest joy in the new heaven and new earth is that God's servants will look upon His face (Rev. 22:4). A prayer movement for spiritual awakening is ultimately asking God to reveal His face—His glory—to the Church and to the world.

Zechariah understood that spiritual awakening was the greatest need for the remnant even in his day, and he knew the answer was God's alone to give. So he called on them to seek God's face in prayer.

Hallmark: The Impact

This prayer movement was not for Israel alone. Ultimately many peoples, cities, nations, and languages would get into the act. As a result of a few vulnerable exiles rebuilding a broken-down Temple and city, God would invade their midst in such a way that many strong nations would come to seek His face.

This would not be a casual turning to the Lord. The pressure would be so great that each of the pray-ers would find people grabbing hold of their clothes, refusing to let go until they were shown the way to salvation.

Some theologians suggest that evangelism in the Old Testament is centrifugal: nations come to Jerusalem to learn of God's salvation. In contrast, they see a centripetal evangelism in the New Testament: God's people move out from Jerusalem to the ends of the earth to declare His salvation. However, Zechariah 8:23 appears to incorporate both approaches. God's glory revealed among His people would give *credibility* to His saving word and draw the nations to Him (centripetal). But the overflow of revival would deploy many of the pray-ers out among various nations, thus making God's saving Word *accessible* worldwide (centrifugal).

In the New Testament we also find this same two-edged approach to evangelism. The international Church, which was formed out of prayer in Jerusalem in the early part of Acts, succeeded as much by its testimony to the Spirit's presence, which brought the fear of the Lord on all citizens, as it did by the apostles' preaching before crowds and the Sanhedrin.

And Paul suggests, in 1 Corinthians 14, that unbelievers drawn into a local congregation in Corinth might be won to Christ as the people proclaim the message of God in unity. "He will fall down and worship God, exclaiming, 'God is really among you!'" (14:24-25). Peter assures us that, along with declaring Christ's excellencies, living together in a godly fashion will force pagans to acknowledge the goodness of our deeds and give glory to God from whom they spring (1 Pet. 2:12).

Hallmark: The Ignition

So where does such a movement of prayer begin? Zechariah's answer is simple: from one person going to another. Those who are still seeking call others to come and seek with them. This is not a groundswell of spiritual elitism. It is not one believer going to another believer to say, "I have found a new, deep experience with God and, if you let me help you, I can show you how to find it, too." Instead, one person and then one group goes to another and says: "We sense God is preparing to do a deep and wonderful work in our generation—look at the visions Zechariah showed us—and that as He does this, all the earth will see His glory as never before. But unless He meets us as His people in a new way, to fulfill His promises and reveal Himself to us, we can do nothing.

"Because we love him so much, we're not willing to sit idly, content with the status quo. We're ready to start seeking Him, and we don't plan to quit until we find all He has for us. In fact, we have no other option. We're desperate to know Him! But we don't want to seek alone. *All* of us need to see His face together. Why don't you come, since you're as desperate as we are, and let's go seek Him together?"

There are two sides to igniting a prayer movement. "Let *us* go" means "we must not pray alone." But, "I myself am going" means "we are so convinced of the need for prayer that even if no one else goes, we will still set the pace and press on to seek God's face."

And so Zechariah's prayer movement grows. One city goes to another, which, at first, may mean nothing more than one family going to another. But soon whole communities are calling each other to revival prayer until, finally, whole nations are carried along in concerted intercession.

Someone must get it started, however. And without the determined few who initially lead the way, it is doubtful if any prayer movement of the magnitude envisioned by Zechariah could ever be hoped for.

"LET US GO AT ONCE!"

Surely the time has come to reestablish a movement of concerted prayer characterized by the hallmarks of grace and promise given us by Zechariah.

God is jealous. He is ready to return and work spiritual awakening among us. He is waiting to show us the face of Christ as we have not seen Him before, that together we might reveal His face before the nations. What are we do do?

One of us needs to go to the other and say, "Come, let us go at once and seek the face of the Lord." Maybe your Bible study group or Christian fellowship might go to another in your church or your campus movement and say, "Come, let us go at once." Maybe you could meet together once a quarter or once every other month or for 10 minutes after a worship service each week to spend time in prayer just for spiritual awakening. Or maybe one Sunday School class could go to another and say, "Once a month let's set aside our Sunday School lesson and gather our two classes together to spend the hour in concerted prayer for spiritual awakening."

Could it possibly come to the time when, as Zechariah suggests, one nation would go to another and say, "Come, let us seek the Lord"? Can you see Madras going to Boston, the Churches in Chicago going to Churches in Sydney, believers in Buenos Aires going to believers in Berlin, Syracuse to Soweto, Hong Kong to London, even believers in Cairo extending the invitation to believers in Jerusalem? Actually, the International Prayer Assembly in 1984 opened the way for this kind of involvement in a fashion unique in history.

Yes, Zechariah's message strongly applies to us today. Through him, God is saying to us all that our duty is to so believe His promises of things to come through Jesus Christ that we unite in a continual attitude of waiting, looking, longing, and seeking. Zechariah invites ordinary people like us to the threshold of spiritual awakening. He shows us that concerted prayer to that end is the frontline in world evangelization. And he makes our effort so simple—we must seek only one thing—to see the face of God.

The face of God revealed to the world—that is what we're praying toward. Church historians describe it in a metaphorical phrase: spiritual awakening. What does that term mean? Let's focus on it next.

4
BEYOND THE THRESHOLD
The Hope Toward Which We Pray

In fulfilling world evangelization, it may surprise you that our first target in prayer is *not* to pray for more missionaries! How can this be when hundreds of thousands more are needed from the church worldwide?

In Matthew 9:35-38, Jesus instructs us to pray for "laborers" to be sent forth by the Lord of the harvest because there are so few to work in the ripened fields. It is apparent that the laborers Jesus had in mind were men and women who had been awakened to the central message of His ministry: that the Kingdom of God was bearing down on their generation. God's promises through the prophets were about to take shape. It was time to wake up, repent and believe the good news about the Promised One, Jesus. In turn, God would "throw out" (literal Greek meaning in 9:38) these revived ones to bring others with them into God's awakening work among His people—to rally God's harassed sheep back to the sovereign Shepherd they were seeking for, to harvest the potential of God's people for serving His

Kingdom, gathering them through renewing fires into God's eternal purposes (cf. Luke 3:16-18).

SPIRITUAL AWAKENING: WHAT IS IT? WHO NEEDS IT?

In our concern for the world, or for a new missionary thrust, what Jesus calls us to pray for first of all, then, is spiritual awakening that begins with a few and spreads to the many, flowing out of prayer and borne along by the preaching of God's Son. We need laborers who gather the Church to seek a full revelation of Jesus Himself, the One in whom God's Kingdom is coming with mysterious but unstoppable force, first among His people and then to the ends of the earth.

From my studies of Scripture and history and from my extended conversations with others, I would like to suggest my own definition of spiritual awakening:

> *Spiritual awakening:* when the Father wakes us up to see Christ's fullness in new ways, so that together we trust Him, love Him, and obey Him in new ways, so that we move with Him in new ways for the fulfillment of His global cause.

Do you recall waking up this morning? Maybe it began with the clamor of the alarm clock, followed by the pitter-patter of feet outside your bedroom. Your eyelids barely budge, however.

Still, you were half conscious of light streaming through the venetian blinds, as you caught the aroma of bacon and eggs. (Collegians: here you might substitute the smell of your roommate's dirty laundry in the closet.) As you lay there, thoughts about the day's activities and responsibilities started to press in on you until, with your eyes half open, you reached the point of no return. Enough awareness invaded your consciousness that you realized it was best to get out of bed, get into your clothes, and get on with the day. You were finally awake!

That's a picture of what happens when God gives spiritual awakening to His Church. Enough of the person of Christ, His glory, and His kingdom—as well as the great needs of His world and our responsibilities to it—invades our consciousness until we are unable to sleep any longer. We awake to get on with God's redemptive purposes for the earth. We have to get up, clothe ourselves in the Lord Jesus Christ, get out the door, and get with the day . . . with *His* day (Rom. 13:11-14). As Paul says in Ephesians 5:14, "Wake up, O sleeper, rise from the dead [sounds like 'get out of bed!'], and Christ will shine on you."

His words remind me of Isaiah 60:1-3: "Arise, shine, for your light has come, and the glory of the Lord rises upon you. See, darkness covers the earth and thick darkness is over the peoples, but the Lord rises upon you and his glory appears over you. Nations will come to your light, and kings to the brightness of your dawn."

Doesn't that sound like getting up in the morning? Jesus uses this image with the Asian churches He addresses in Revelation 2 and 3. For example, to the church at Sardis He says: "I know your deeds; you have a reputation of being alive, but you are dead. *Wake up!* Strengthen what remains and is about to die, for I have not found your deeds complete in the sight of my God" (3:1-2, italics added). And with the church at Laodicea, Jesus is so hidden to their hardened hearts that it is as if He is on the outside of the church, asking permission to enter again and to offer salve for their blind eyes.

Paul had the same concern in mind when he prayed in his Epistles. In fact, whenever God fully answers the written prayers of Paul for any church or the whole Church in any generation, revival results!

Take for example, his prayer for the Ephesians; "I keep asking that the God of our Lord Jesus Christ, the glorious Father, may give you the Spirit of wisdom and revelation, so that you may know him better. I pray also that the eyes of your heart may be enlightened that you may know the hope to which he has called you, the riches of his glorious inheritance in the saints, and his incomparably great power for us who believe" (Eph. 1:17-19). A spirit of revelation, knowing God better, our heart's eyes enlightened, a new vision of our hope, inheritance and power—this is spiritual awakening.

Spiritual awakening is both a process and an event. In a sense, the whole process of Christian growth is awakening. It's a rapid series of mini-revivals in which at any given point one can

say: "I am committing all I can see of myself to all I can see of
Christ for all I can see of His global cause—at this moment."
Since the Spirit daily reveals to us more of Christ, of ourselves,
and of God's plans for the world, *every* new insight that leads to a
new act of obedience can be called spiritual awakening.

Our insistence then is on knowing Christ, knowing who we
are in Christ, and knowing how best to serve His global cause.
Hebrews 11:6 describes those who desire to know more of our
Lord, of His plans and purposes for us and for the world as those
who "earnestly seek him." Seeking and finding is an unending
process, like an upward spiral.

Two words have helped me to pinpoint the distinctiveness of
spiritual awakening as an event, in its more technical, biblical-
historical sense: The words are "intensify" and "accelerate." In
times of broader spiritual awakening, God intensifies the
Church's relationship with Christ and He accelerates the
advancement of Christ's Kingdom through the Church.

Using my definition, let's study spiritual awakening as an
event while breaking it down into five parts:
1. When the Father wakes us up;
2. To see the fullness of Christ in new ways;
3. To trust, love, and obey Him in new ways;
4. To move with Him in new ways for the fulfillment of His
global cause; and
5. Together.

When the Father Wakes Us Up

Spiritual awakening comes at God's gracious initiative. And
we are totally dependent upon Him for it. That's why we must
make it our target in prayer, so that we may see Christ in new
ways. Even prayer is a gift of God. As A.W. Tozer reminds us in
The Pursuit of God, when we feel stirred to seek after Christ,
"God is always previous."

Without exception, true revival is that which is only attribut-
able to the Father. He is responsible for a heavenly invasion in
the affairs of the Church, and is directly involved at every point.
In spiritual awakening, He activates a bold strategy to bring us
into intimacy with Himself and His redemptive mission to the
nations through an unveiling of Christ's presence in our midst.

Those who have studied it suggest that the fear of the Lord is at the heart of revival. The more vividly God shows us Himself and His purposes in Christ, the more seriously we are driven to take both our fellowship with Him and our commission from Him. The Church is reintroduced to the consuming Fire from heaven and tastes His holy love with trembling obedience. The Spirit of the Lord revives our corporate sense of Christ's intimate direction of both our inward and outward life.

In our parable of the threshold, it was the light through the partially-opened door that drew any of us to knock in the first place. Yes, God is previous. He wakes us up.

To See Christ's Fullness in New Ways

Spiritual awakening will never take us beyond Jesus. He is what awakening is all about. God does not possess anything beyond Christ to give to His people. Jesus exhausts for all of us all we can ever know of God, all we can ever receive from God, and all we can ever become for God. The Puritans said, "We can't be in union with half of Christ." In spiritual awakening, God brings us back to the whole Christ.

You have probably heard the phrase "a pouring out of the Spirit" in reference to revival. Where does that fit in? Precisely at the point of revealing the fullness of Christ and the gospel.

Of course, it is possible to pray for the Spirit's outpouring and really be asking God to bless and empower only what we have previously determined to do. But in its proper and biblical use, the Spirit's outpouring results in our seeing and embracing all we have in Christ, and responding in love to all He tells us to do.

In reality, the Spirit does not come down to us at all. He came down at Pentecost and now indwells His whole Church. Awakening is more like our total cooperation with His unrelentingly glorious ministry of taking the things of Christ and declaring them to us (John 16:14). His ministry is not to speak of Himself. He wants Christ to be glorified before us and through us. "By illuminating our minds, and by softening our hard hearts, by guiding and strengthening our wills, the Spirit leads us into an increasing experience of the deliverance that Christ won for us."[6]

This work of the Spirit blossoms in awakening. The Spirit brings within our reach an apprehension of Christ comparable to the deepest needs of the Church of that particular generation and to the outward challenge to her worldwide mission.

To Trust, Love and Obey Him in New Ways

Once the Father invades our midst, giving His children new eyes to see Christ's fullness in new ways, a response emerges from the Church that can ultimately affect the whole earth and change the course of history. George Whitefield wrote of his own experience in awakenings: "My understanding was enlightened, my will broken, and my affections more and more enlivened with zeal for Christ." This zeal is best expressed in three simple words: trust, love, obey.

First, we learn to *trust* Christ in new ways. Having become newly impressed with both the supremacy and sufficiency of Christ, the Holy Spirit confronts us with specifics regarding how we propose to respond to the Lordship of Jesus. In revival, He intensifies His probings: Is Christ Lord of heaven and earth? Does He stand at the climax of history? Is He the one at whose feet the nations will come out for disposal? Is He Lord of the Church? Is He Lord through the Church to fulfill His purposes for all peoples and bring all of life under the rule of His Kingdom? Is He Lord of my life? Does He have the right to my allegiance, my obedience, and my love? Am I prepared to give all to Christ, without reservations, without strings attached, and without deceit?

Such a faith will not stand alone. It leads to love, and love leads to obedience. Just as faith takes on new dimensions in spiritual awakening, so love and obedience accelerate. We come to *love* Christ in new ways simply because He stops being a stranger. We have a vivid experience with Christ that springs from faith because our relationship with Him has been heightened and intensified. Some would say that awakening overwhelms us with Christ, taking us out of ourselves and into devotion to Him. After all, as Paul teaches in Galatians 5, our faith in Him will increasingly work itself out in love.

And love gives birth to *obedience*. Awakening is not only a profound new experience with Christ, it is also a time for plain "guts." When Jesus calls us to follow Him and lose our lives for His sake and the gospel's, He is talking about sacrificial obedience. Awakening helps the Church accelerate in its knowledge of Christ which, in the original language, means to grow in our "caring" for Christ and the things of Christ. And caring changes the direction of our affections so that we willingly give Him obedience in a love that knows no limits. That is gutsy stuff!

I remember seeing an ad for an airlines. Under a full-page photo of an attractive young flight attendant with a magnetic smile was the caption: "If you're wondering where all this comes from, well, it comes from inside. Our people are happy. Because they love what they do and who they do it for. When people feel that way, they simply have more to give . . . . "

Just so, as God brings us to know Christ's love in new ways because we see Him in new ways, we are set free to obediently give love to others in new ways whether in the form of a smile, a bank check, a word of encouragement, or our very lives. In awakening, we encounter the heart of the universe, which is nothing less than sacrificial love, and as we obey Him He leads us to the same expression of love. As we learn to know the presence of God in all of His gifts of love, we become willing to abandon ourselves for His purposes of love.

This demonstration of faith through love and obedience is what I call "decisive devotion," a devotion that is a single-minded giving of ourselves to Christ. We trust Him and love Him so much that our thoughts, our words, our relationships, and the directions we move with Him are centered on the fulfillment of everything that is on His heart.

The ultimate goal of awakening is decisive devotion to Christ, manifested in three ways: (1) Our highest passion becomes Christ Himself, that we may know Him and that others may know and love Him with us; (2) our highest purpose becomes the advancement of Christ's Kingdom by the impact of the gospel, for this is how all people can join us to know and love Him for who He is; and, (3) our highest priority increasingly becomes the unreached and unliberated of the earth, who are unresponsive and unaware of the gospel and, therefore, unclaimed for Christ's Kingdom and unable to love and serve Him at all.

To Move with Him in the Fulfillment of
His Global Cause

Two words that have helped me understand the scope of spiritual awakening are "fullness" and "fulfillment." Both words are used in the definition we're exploring here. As we've seen, fullness speaks of everything that God is and offers to us in His Son. Christ is the fullness of the Godhead in bodily form, in whom we have come to fullness of life (Col. 2:9-10).

Fulfillment points *not* to personal fulfillment (except indirectly), but rather to the fulfillment of all that is on the heart of God—His work through a revived Church to bring the fullness of Christ to the attention of the nations in the advancement of His Kingdom. Without such fulfillment, revival will stagnate in the shallows of selfish ambition.

Spiritual awakening in the Church holds the promise of spiritual awakening among the nations. When God blesses us in awakening it is so that we might become a blessing to the families of the earth (Gen. 12:2-3). The more He engages us with His son, the more He wants us to move with Christ to fulfill His global cause.

As we accept the offer to see Christ's fullness and pursue it, we submit our lives to Him at the same time to be broken and reshaped to fit wherever and however we may best serve His global cause. Does this hold similarities to the threshold parable in chapter 1? In one sense, it is the other side of that story.

If revival does not enhance His glory and advance His Kingdom throughout the earth, it needs to be questioned. Sometimes we can even shape revival into an idol and worship it as a way to achieve our own objectives or feather our own nests. How foolilsh we can be. Revival is no shortcut to the blessings of being a heavenly saint; rather, it opens the long road to the blessings and sufferings of being Christ's earthly servant. As Anglican missions statesman Max Warren reminds us: "Awakening is a reformation of the Church for action."

I see awakening in five natural phases:

1. The Spirit of God raises up a movement of united prayer for revival.

2. In response to prayer, the Church receives an intensified vision of Christ's fullness.

3. As a result, the Church is led into a deep unity of love for one another and a resolve to serve the purposes of Christ together.

4. From this springs up a revitalization and a pruning of existing ministries.

5. All of this flows into an expansion of Christ's Kingdom with international repercussions.

What I have discovered is that, like waves washing higher and higher on a beach, spiritual awakening accelerates the impact of Christ's lordship not only in the life of the Church, but also in society, and among the nations, and at many levels.

In an awakening today we can expect the Kingdom to extend its influence as the Church moves forward in obedience. Marriages will be healed and homes restored. The crime rate will drop, often dramatically. A spirit of generosity and sacrificial giving will increase. Christian influence will be brought to bear on the media and on institutions of higher learning. Christ's lordship will be explored in many spheres: care of the environment, concern for the unemployed, the humane treatment of employees, honesty in work, and advocacy for the disadvantaged. Society will become infused with dedicated love and practical justice. Social and moral legislation will emerge as the Church gains renewed sensitivity to the poor and disenfranchised. The Church will learn to know how powerful Jesus is as she sees Him at work through her in the lives of the powerless. And peacemaking among the nations will become a growing concern of leaders in lands where spiritual awakening has flowed.

So That . . . Together

Although awakening may be an individual experience, God intends it ultimately to be corporate.

Revival accelerates our commitment to the Church because what we think of Christ and what we think of His Church go hand-in-hand. The more we love Christ and the more we see of Him in an awakened Church—that is, the more we see of Him in each other—the more we will desire to give ourselves to one another for Jesus' sake.

In revival God intensifies all the gifts already within the Body and allows them to overflow with the fullness of Christ. According to Ephesians 4, it's impossible to enter into the fullness of Christ until the spiritual gifts are set free, made available, and activated. Consider the covenant or small group that you may be a part of right now. What if God gave awakening to your group so that you were set free not only to serve one another but also to seek out a ministry together to the world around you? Would that derail what you originally envisioned for your group when it formed? Of course not. It would complete your purpose. Now expand that proposition to your local church, and to the Church at large. You see, being "together" is a critical part of both entering into awakening and bringing forth its fruits.

CONCLUSION: GANDHI AND AWAKENING

As I sat captivated by the Academy Award-winning film *Gandhi*, I thought of revival. Why? Because I saw the life of a man who, though not committed to the King, lived out with determination many of the principles Jesus taught as basic building blocks of the Kingdom. As a result of his unyielding adherence to such principles as simplicity, humility, identity with the poor, love of enemies, and vicarious suffering, the life of this one man, Gandhi, transformed the face of India and redirected the twentieth century.

Watching the movie I thought to myself: What if God were to revive His people with renewed, decisive devotion to the King? What if the whole Church, or at least a large segment of it, would awaken to the principle of the Kingdom in uncompromising obedience in union with the King? Considering what one human sinner with a few divine truths accomplished on his own, could a revived Church leave the world the same? Would there not come forth a dramatic fulfillment of Christ's global cause that would be unstoppable? Would we not see the knowledge of the glory of Christ covering the earth "as the waters cover the sea" (Hab. 2:14)?

Spiritual awakening, then, is the strategic target for concerted prayer. Again, spiritual awakening is "when the Father wakes us up to see Christ's fullness in new ways, so that together we trust Him, love Him, and obey Him in new ways, so that we move with Him in new ways for the fulfillment of His global cause." A movement of prayer that focuses on this is never parochial; in every respect it is a movement of prayer for the world. Concerted prayer for spiritual awakening is the most critical step the church can take for the sake of the nation.

That leaves us, however, with one important question: Do we have any reason to believe that ours is a generation in which God would be pleased to grant spiritual awakening to a Church united in prayer to seek Him in it? Is there hope?

The answer to that should encourage us all.

5

SPIRITUAL AWAKENING
Four Good Reasons to Look for It!

If we want to assist concerts of prayer where we live, we must grasp the vision of what we are praying toward, which will then motivate and help us to endure until God answers. You see, there are four reasons for us to expect a spiritual awakening and to pray hopefully toward it:

Reason 1—The Divine Pattern
Reason 2—The Dark Prospects
Reason 3—The Disturbing Paralysis
Reason 4—The Dramatic Preparations

Reason 1
THE DIVINE PATTERN

With our Father, awakening and revival are a way of life. During the least promising of times, He has always had a people of prayer, full of faith that He would re-awaken His Church with international repercussions. What kept them praying? They believed: "God has done it before, surely He is willing and able to do it again, even in our generation."

I was hit with His pattern by an experiment I recently conducted. Taking an inexpensive copy of the Bible, I worked through it from Genesis to Revelation looking for verses on awakening. I marked each one I found with a yellow highlighting pen. Then I thumbed back through the pages for the results. Do

you know what? Almost half my Bible was yellow! There wa
that much in it on God's renewing, restoring, recovering, reviv
ing His people. And there were hundreds of other verses on His
redeeming purposes for *all* nations, often advanced as a result of
revival. I haven't prayed the same since.

I found that the Old Testament emphasizes why awakening
and restoration are necessary and why they are critically tied to
the worldwide impact of God's Kingdom. The New Testament
describes in what forms a full awakening occurs.

Surveying the past 2,000 years helps us uncover the diverse
drama of this biblical pattern. It's like studying the changing
shafts of light from a masterfully cut diamond. We're left with
great encouragement for any movement of prayer. If God has
revived His people before, He is willing and able to do it again,
even in our generation. Some church historians suggest that
past awakenings are like dress rehearsals for a reviving work
which God is preparing to unfold today.

Reason 2
THE DARK PROSPECTS

In 1983, Aleksandr Solzhenitsyn observed, "Today's world
has reached a stage that, if it had been described to preceding
centuries, it would have called forth the cry: 'this is apoca-
lypse.'" In his recent best-seller, *Approaching Hoofbeats,* Billy
Graham writes: "There is something ominous in the air and my
bones vibrate with the horror of it."

I want to explore some current global nightmares—not to
depress you but to convince you that we must cry to God in
prayer. Awakenings have often occurred during the world's
darkest hours. Frankly, the situation today is bad enough that
there's little question God must intervene, either in judgment
because our rebellion has gone too far, or in a global-sized work
of grace as He rains mercy down on us all. And there is every
reason to believe that if we cry for mercy, it will be ours! For if
God doesn't give awakening, the world has no other hopeful
prospect.

The Unreached: Six Million Beachheads to Go

The numbers of unreached people are staggering. There are

as many people in the world who have no knowledge of Christ as the number of times your heart will beat from the day you were born to the day you reach 75—at least 2.5 billion strong. This does not include, of course, the hundreds of millions of nominal Christians in the world who have yet to come to true saving faith in Christ. Nor does it include the one billion non-Christians who could be reached through regular evangelism by Christians around the world who are like them culturally, socially and linguistically. No, we're talking about 2.5 billion people who can be reached only by major new cross-cultural efforts in love and communication.

Obviously, then, the complexity of the task is just as overwhelming as the numbers involved. There are tremendous roadblocks to the gospel within the diverse human family. Throughout the world, awesome boundaries—geographical, social, economic, political, cultural, linguistic, religious, racial, generational, and even physical—cut human beings off from one another. Some estimate as many as 20,000 distinct people groupings throughout the world—some with as few as 9,000 members, like a tribe in Nigeria; others with as many as 30 million, like a caste in India—where there's no inborn evangelizing community of Christians among them. Most of the time, they're in need of outside, cross-cultural assistance if they are ever to come to Christ.

The world can be evangelized effectively only by a Church so thoroughly revived that we begin sacrificially to multiply determined, equipped, Spirit-filled, cross-cultural servants of the gospel. If we were to pray that God would give the earth one actively ministering congregation for every 1,000 people in the world—a ratio that insures adequate resources for ministry to the whole person, approximately six million new churches would be needed among non-Christians or nominal Christians by the year 2000. It would also require 600,000 additional intercultural workers from the Church worldwide. If that doesn't call for extraordinary divine intervention on behalf of the nations, I don't know what does!

Population Explosion: Where's Your Calculator?
There are more people alive today than ever died in all of

human history! Every five days, another one million people are added to our planet. At the end of 1982, the world registered its biggest 12-month population increase in history: 84 million people.

In 1983, 4.7 billion people inhabited the earth. By 1990 that number will rise to 5.3 billion; by the middle of the next century, we will have 9 billion inhabitants. Most of the growth will take place in the less developed world. Today, 10 of every 11 babies are born in the Third World. With most of the unreached currently in Africa and Asia, what will it mean to have 75 percent of our planet's people residing there within two decades?

With all of these sobering statistics staring us in the face, we realize that the Church entering the twenty-first century faces a larger number of people to be loved and reached for Jesus Christ than ever before.

Population Implosion: Can Anyone Pry Us Apart?

"Population implosion" occurs when more and more people are jammed into smaller and smaller areas. Today there is a massive movement of our growing population from the country to the city, referred to as urbanization.

Sociologists talk of "world class cities," those that have one million people or more. The number of these cities should double by the year 2000, with almost 300 cities of one million and 70 of two million or more. As we move toward the twenty-first century, 75 percent of Third World population will live in urban settings. For the first time in history, a majority of the world's urban dwellers will be found in the Third World. These urban centers often become, in Ray Bakke's terms, "the throw away place" for an upwardly and outwardly migrating middle class, and a caldron of unfulfilled expectations and frustrations for newly arrived, usually unskilled minorities. Theodore White calls our cities "warehouses for the very poor or enclaves for the very rich."

What does this urbanization mean for evangelization and a movement of prayer for the world? For one thing, it's a fact that where the cities go, the nations go, and so goes the world. So, unless Christians successfully confront the major urban problems of our day, we will soon face unfathomable difficulties in preaching the gospel, and we'll be up against cultural and moral forces undreamed of today. Are there any hopeful prospects unless God powerfully intervenes to mobilize His Church?

Poverty: A Brutality That Lasts and Lasts

The more settled and secure our daily experiences are, the harder it is for us to imagine the brutality of poverty that so much of the world experiences. Almost one billion people survive on a per capita income of $75 a year (I just paid that much for a summer blazer!). No wonder they spend most of their time simply worrying about survival.

In India, as many as 300 million people concentrate their limited physical energy on securing one bowl of rice each day. The number of hopelessly poor worldwide is increasing at a rate faster than total population. By the year 2000, an estimated one billion people will be among the landless, hopelessly poor.

It is critical that the Church move immediately from any passive analysis of the hungry and dispossessed. Unitedly, we must ask the Lord to awaken us to the fullness of Christ so that out of His love and our obedience to Him, we might respond with repentance, justice, and compassion to earth's poor, most of whom are also unreached.

Technocracy: The Empire Strikes Fast!

The arena of technology presents us with a "good news-bad news" situation. The good news is that much of what's being developed can be harnessed for the furtherance of the gospel. The bad news is that much of it could create global nightmares that make *Star Wars* look like a bedtime story.

The dominance of technology, sometimes called "technocracy," can lead, for example, to increased possibilities for surveillance and control of others. We face genetic engineering, which allows us the possibility of playing God with other people's lives. When we control the genetic makeup and even the direction of a person's future, we exercise ultimate power over another human.

The information revolution—the availability of instant information—will have impact well beyond upheavals of the Industrial Revolution. Once knowledge was truth; today knowledge has become power. As a result, social scientists are predicting the emergence of a new class of citizens within every nation and sometimes including whole nations: the "information poor," those who are unable to become part of the information age. This can only exaccerbate their already desperate economic plight.

The Church must lead the way to the understanding of true biblical values and their relationship to technological powers and dangers. As the Church harnesses technology for the advance of the Kingdom, it must also have the heart to use technology to serve a world that is suffering and lost and to facilitate the obedience of faith among the nations. Surely this is what our Father would desire for us. Unless He revives the hearts of Christians to care and respond, the world is vulnerable to a technocratic empire that may strike back at us with a fury.

Militarism: Road to Armaggedon?

Will there even *be* a world to evangelize by the year 2000? It's a sobering but valid question, posed with the greatest urgency. And the prospects are dark indeed.

The governments of the world are turning us into a massive armed camp. In 1976, world military expenditures exceeded $350 billion. Just eight years later that figure soared to more than $600 billion. At $1 million a minute, the world today spends twice as much on defense as it spends on food, and five times as much as it spends on housing.

What if the Church does not find a convincingly renewed life under the Lord Jesus to boldly confront the fear, aggression, and insane plotting that brings forth this potential destruction? And what if we don't awaken to stand together as a people who genuinely demonstrate by word, deed, and policy that Christ, not the bomb, is our refuge and our Lord? I'm afraid we will have little spiritual power to preach the Good News of reconciliation with effect among the earth's unreached, even if they survive to hear us and we to tell them.

It is in this desperate situation that we find the greatest hope that God is ready to respond in mercy to a movement of prayer toward spiritual awakening. We also find every good reason in this to get about the business of praying.

Competition· Buffeted by Seas of Doctrine

Without an awakening we face other dark prospects due to the increased intensity of ideological forces that oppose the advancement of the gospel.

For example, secularism claims, "Whatever can be accomplished through human resources is all that there is." As a world view it presents a deadly clash with the gospel. Humanism, the fruit of secularization, declares humankind to be the final authority in everything. The world's universities, which have largely surrendered active concern over the realities of spirit and of revelation, are saturated with humanism. There seems to be no strong regard for fixed truth or values. Instead there's an accommodation to many views as the special triumph of modern man.

The Church is also buffeted by seas of *competing religions.* When it comes to the penetration of the gospel among the great world religions, the prospects seem dark indeed. For example, we've watched a great upsurge in Buddhism since World War II. There are more than 500 million Buddhists worldwide. Despite its idolatry and superstitious darkness, Hinduism is experiencing its own mass awakening. Much of this "awakening" has been carried out at great personal sacrifice on the part of workers who go forth to preach Hinduism and to the many who, out of a meager income, support those who go.

It seems that the Church worldwide will shortly be engulfed by these waves of sophisticated doctrine unless God convinces the nations with irrefutable clarity that Jesus is Lord and that He is in the midst of His people as the hope of the world (Colossians 1:27). Toward that miracle, concerted prayer must move; by that hopeful vision concerted prayer will be sustained.

The Greatest Conspiracy

Ultimately, however, we face the overwhelming nightmare found in every generation: the condition of humankind's heart. The fifty-dollar term theologians use is "total depravity." There are enough dark prospects in this nightmare alone to compel a movement of prayer.

It is not that we humans are entirely bad—we are able to paint beautiful paintings or engage in a variety of philanthropic works if we choose—but our desire to know God and to pursue

all of our legitimate goals in order to please Him, is, in David
Hubbard's words, stone cold. All people are lawless, rebellious,
and wicked. This rebellion goes beyond rebellious acts to rebellious intentions, attitudes, alliances, and allegiances.

But there is an added dimension to this. We are told that the
whole world of sinners lies in the hands "of the evil one" (1 John
5:19). A conspiracy is active right now against the Kingdom of
God, and its leader is alive and working feverishly on earth. The
temptations, oppressions, and persecutions we often experience in the world missionary thrust come at this point. We
aggressively operate in the whirlpool ultimately created, not by
scarcity, technology or war, but by the convergence of two diametrically opposed spiritual powers, one who knows his time is
very short and One who is assured of ultimate victory.

The more oppressive Satan makes the world's night, the
greater our hope that we in the Church are near the dawn of a
new era of spiritual awakening. Our King will not be defeated! In
a movement of prayer we rally toward His coming triumph, we
forcefully advance His Kingdom against all foes.

Reason 3
OUR DISTURBING PARALYSIS

Next, we turn to the wonder and mystery of the American
evangelical movement—the wonder of its potential for serving
Christ's Kingdom and the mystery of its paralysis to activate
spiritual dynamics that comprehensively transform our nation
and the world. Its expression in America is a case in point.

We might call the latter a "paralysis of faith." It focuses on
nightmares closer to home and represents the third major reason for the need of awakening. For if God doesn't revive us, the
Church may have no other way out of its paralysis.

A Visibly Thriving Enterprise

Something quite significant is definitely happening. Our God-
given potential is showing. A look at the ferment in our churches
proves we must be doing more than just daydreaming. In the
United States at least 40 million of us—nearly one out of every
five adults—are evangelicals. What difference does that make?

In general, studies conclude that evangelicals contribute

more generously to the Church, understand their faith better, and are more ready to speak of it to others. American evangelicals are strongly Bible-centered in their faith, and seek to be faithful to Scripture, convinced the Bible is God's Word. Recent surveys show that 85 percent of North American protestants are absolutely certain Scripture is the "revealed word of God." Eighty-five percent of U.S. evangelicals dip into the Scriptures at least weekly, almost half every day.

If one measure of spiritual vitality is church membership, note that in 1981 church membership stood at 138,452,614, an increase of almost 4 million over 10 years before. Today there are 370,000 churches in the United States to service this growing interest. It's no surprise then, that outwardly evangelicalism appears to be a thriving enterprise.

Over the past 10 years, evangelical churches have posted record gains and have also increased political clout. They've taken on crusades as never before on a variety of issues including abortion, homosexuality, the role of women, the plight of the poor, and the reformation of national morality.

Vitality can also be seen in the growth of the charismatic renewal movement which, though a worldwide phenomenon, has its largest following in the United States. In 1980, a Gallup poll concluded that 29 million evangelicals also call themselves charismatic. The charismatic movement has penetrated every denomination, with its most significant dimension within the Roman Catholic Church.

Evangelical books now account for a third of the total domestic commercial book sales. More than 1,300 radio stations and dozens of television stations devote all or most of their time to religious broadcasting. We have multiplied what many call parachurch organizations, providing a plethora of ways for evangelicals to obey the Great Commission. Over 1,000 organizations are members of the National Religious Broadcasters, while over 30 nationwide campus ministries are seeking to penetrate both Christian and secular campuses. In responding to the world beyond our shores, the American evangelical movement has fostered over 700 overseas ministries, many of which have appeared within the past 30 years.

What are we to make of this kaleidoscope of activity and

energy? Richard Lovelace calls it a "steadily increasing displacement of the works of darkness" and suggests that it may appropriately be called a revival in a biblical sense. If that's true, it leaves me with hope of more to come.

The Paralysis of American Evangelicalism

Yet everywhere I go, in my discussions with evangelical leaders, it appears that despite all this, something is not quite right. As theologian Louis Drummond remarks on current evangelical renewal: "It simply has missed the bulk of God's people. And that is the prime problem!"

Having spent time with Senate Chaplain Richard Halverson, I understand his concern expressed in an interview with *Eternity* magazine:

> I believe we're on the threshold of something happening that is going to be as great or greater than the Reformation . . . I feel that we are a lot farther into it than we realize . . . (But) I am deeply concerned about the acculturation of evangelicals. They are infected by a very subtle worldliness—materialism and comfort in this world. I have been concerned about the pragmatism—the quantification of everything: numbers, bigness, television success, buildings. It is as though quality has nothing to do with growth . . . with all the growing evangelicalism—the talk of spiritual awakening—our social order continues to deteriorate.[1]

In one of his last editorials for *Christianity Today*, Dr. Kenneth Kantzer concurred. Looking at the potency of evangelicalism in 1983 and beyond, he raised serious questions about the depth of its influence on our nation: "Evangelicalism is weaker now than it was fifteen years ago, or fifty years ago. The influence of evangelical faith and evangelical ethics is less. As a culture, our nation and, indeed western Europe, are moving away from biblical Christianity. Most people don't realize that one hundred years ago the mainline denominations were all evangelical."[2]

Of course, there are reasonable explanations for this paralysis. The immensity and complexity of reaching our world for Christ, as well as the uncertainties of the task, are almost suffocating. Crushed by forces that plague our society, we freeze to our seats like passive spectators.

On top of all that, many of us are spiritually and psychologically fatigued. Ruth Graham calls the modern evangelical "packed man." We have so many options that we are paralyzed with over-choice and fatigued by trying to carry out too much, too soon, too fast, too often.

Are we unwilling to be involved more deeply in world evangelization? Or are we unable, despite all of our potential? Perhaps we're not so much weary of the work as we are weary in the work. For many, heart exhaustion has set in.

In any case, the present evangelical "revival" appears to have relatively little impact on such issues as crime, racism, poverty, militarism and the general moral climate.

What does the nation think of the evangelical movement? Psychologist John White claims that "because God is not perceived by non-Christians as the power behind the success, success may be only partial and be thought of as being no different from that of other clubs and associations."[3] A.W. Tozer said, "Current evangelism has laid the altar and divided the sacrifice into parts, but now seems satisfied to count the stones and rearrange the pieces with never a care that there is not a sign of fire upon top of the lofty Carmel."[4] Our society, failing to see the sign of fire, often turns away disillusioned, skeptical, or bored. Somebody needs to wake up!

Analysis of Paralysis

We can't avoid the facts. The evangelical movement of America is experiencing a disturbing sense of paralysis. Carl Henry wonders if we're "out of the closet but going nowhere?" This paralysis may be the greatest barrier to effective mobilization for world evangelization, as well.

The more we become aware of our paralysis, the more pressure we should sense from the Spirit to seek the face of God in a movement of prayer for spiritual awakening. And that's the beginning of a new day for all of us. It will bring us into the

realms of hope described for another paralyzed generation in
Isaiah 26:17-19:

> As a woman with child and about to give birth
> writhes and cries out in her pain, so were we in your
> presence, O Lord. We were with child, we writhed
> in pain, but we gave birth to wind. We have not
> brought salvation to the earth; we have not given
> birth to the people of the world.
>
> But your dead will live; their bodies will rise. You
> who dwell in the dust, wake up and shout for joy.
> Your dew is like the dew of the morning; the earth
> will give birth to her dead.

No matter how thwarted we evangelicals may feel in our
impact on society or the nations, we can still rejoice in our God-
given potential for the Kingdom—if we simply become a Church
at prayer for revival—ordinary people at the threshold.

Reason 4
THE DRAMATIC PREPARATIONS

Woody Allen satirizes, "Mankind is caught at a crossroads.
One road leads to hopelessness and despair, and the other leads
to total annihilation. Let us pray we have the wisdom to choose
rightly!" He's hit on one mood of our generation.

But there is another mood abroad. Others have begun to
place hope for global survival squarely in the arena of the human
spirit, in spiritual and moral renaissance. There's a growing cry
for mediators, for those with the intellectual and moral integrity
not just to model the solutions, but to help lead us into those
solutions.

It is critical that the Church ask God to break us out of our
bulwark mentality, our hardness of heart—out of our paralysis of
faith—into the versatility and power of His Kingdom. What an
hour for the Church to rediscover the fullness of Christ as Lord,
and to move with Him in the fulfillment of His global cause! He
can end hostilities between nations. He can lead cultures and
peoples into an experience of redemption and justice. He is the
one able to satisfy the basic longings of the human heart and to

quiet the fears that plague mankind. The world appears to be in preparation to hear the message of Christ as never before!

An examination of some of these preparations suggests that God is building a fireplace, brick by brick, to project the heat and light of His Kingdom to the ends of the earth. But the question we need to ask is, if God is building this fireplace, can the fire of spiritual awakening be very far behind? If God is preparing the Church and the world for revival, should we not expect it to be at hand? And should we all not be praying toward it with electric hope?

International Preparations

The world is being bonded together as never before, preparing the way for God's redemptive action on a magnificent scale.

John Naisbitt suggests that two inventions have played a key role in transforming our planet into a global city: the jet airplane and the communications satellite, with the satellite being the most important of the two. For the first time, we have the capability of instantaneous interaction. Before the close of this decade, our planet will have 1 billion telephones that are so interconnected that it will be possible to call directly to anyone else among the other 1 billion. The amount of time needed to transmit information has been reduced to seconds.

The world faces survival issues that can be addressed effectively only by the Word of God. In bringing these questions unavoidably to the surface, is not the Spirit preparing the way for the life-saving ministry of a Church revived in the fullness of the Lord of Creation? And could our Father be preparing to use this new technology to equip His Church for world evangelization?

What would happen, asks Richard Lovelace, if the whole planet is driven to call upon the name of the Lord, and if the information that is broadcast is that His name is Jesus?

National Preparation

The trends within our own nation also give us compelling reasons to unite in prayer for spiritual awakening. From divine perspective, these are surely dramatic preparations.

The American people face their own crisis of meaning. We know that we are no longer at the center of world history, as we once were. Who are we, we wonder?

We are losing confidence about our future, too. Do we face a future of continued unemployment, recurring cycles of inflation, increasing national debt, and shrinking options for personal fulfillment? By one survey, 50 percent of Americans fret about national and personal prospects.

We have also undergone a serious ethical collapse and an erosion of trust. Theodore White said, "The great issue in America is whether or not, as in the past, Americans can trust each other." A breakdown in natural leadership has helped to accelerate this erosion of trust. Many of us are losing faith in people we once called experts. Pollster Louis Harris notes that the "index of alienation" has climbed steadily from 29 percent in 1966 to 58 percent today. Could this be further preparation for a demonstration of trust and reconciliation displayed by a Church reunited around the glory of Christ (see John 17)?

In the face of all this upheaval and change, other positive preparations are in evidence. A spiritual hunt is underway. Our society is increasingly reaching out for connectedness with the world as we seek closer and deeper personal relationships and turn from the pursuit of things to pursuit of the sacred. Daniel Yankelovich in *New Rules* observes that we're moving toward an "ethic of commitment." Who has stirred up this pursuit?

Pursuit of the Sacred. Our society is far more religious than secularists would have us believe. According to George Gallup, American people as a whole continue to be the most openly religious and traditional of all western societies. Eighty-seven percent of Americans say that Christ has had a moral or ethical influence on their lives, and 81 percent consider Jesus divine. More than three-fourths of Americans say that Jesus is alive and in the heavenly realm and that "He lives in and cares for you."

The soil is being prepared for something unusual. Gallup remarks: "Americans are a people of deep religious roots, roots that when watered with kindness and compassion will once more grow."

Pursuit of the Neighbor. I also see preparation for awakening as Americans look for deeper commitments in their relationships not only to God, but to one another. Often we feel like an aggregate of strangers, a society fragmented by colliding interests. We are in need not only of a sense of common purpose, but also of relationship to one another in achieving that purpose. Yankelovich has found that 40 percent of Americans are currently involved in a search for community. Sociologist Daniel Bell writes of one way we're finding it: "Probably in no other country in the world is there such a high degree of voluntary communal activity." Another social analyst says the demand for therapy is being replaced by a "demand for access to the world."

The Vitality of World Christianity

Pentecostals. Some would claim that the explosion of the Pentecostal movement worldwide is proof that revival has come. Certainly it is one demonstration of vitality in world Christianity, and may be, in the words of Peter Wagner, evidence that we're on "the crest of the wave" in global awakening and outreach. Pentecostal and charismatic churches are growing faster than any other Christian groups with an estimated 65 million. The world's largest churches are Pentecostal, and are found in the Third World: Central Church in Seoul (300,000), Jotabeche Church in Santiago (80,000), and Congregacao Cristo Sao Paulo (62,000). The charismatic movement has reached a vast array of socioeconomic classes throughout the world with the gospel, contextualized in a way that often "fits" Third World cultures most effectively.

If what we see now in many parts of the Church is just the crest of global awakening, then what a glorious floodtide lies ahead. If the current explosion of the Church is but the "sunrise of missions" (Donald McGavran), then what are we and the world ultimately being prepared *for?*

Growing Numbers. More people have become Christians since World War II than in all the rest of church history. The number of Christians worldwide is increasing at a rate of 78,000 a day, with over 1,600 new churches every week. Churches in East Asia and South Asia are growing by 360,000 and 447,000 converts per year, respectively. If the current trend continues, by the year 2000, 60 percent of the world's Christians will live in the Third World.

Of course, it is true that approximately 1 billion of the world's Christians need to be re-evangelized. But this still leaves over 450 million Christians worldwide who are "active" in that they are attending church at least once a week, and at least 250 million are evangelicals. Active evangelical Christians are certainly capable of sharing Christ with their nominal Christian friends in a new and powerful way, as God gives renewed vision of Christ's fullness through awakening. Many of the one billion nominals are just as ready to be released by revival into a genuine saving faith that mobilizes them for the task before us.

Open Doors. Much of the world's population is accessible to Christian witnesses coming from the outside. Within parts of Southeast Asia, the Philippines, Taiwan and Japan, there are as many as 200 million people who can be openly reached with the gospel. Right now there are more than enough open doors to claim the attention of tens of thousands of new missionaries worldwide. Further, research indicates more individuals and segments of populations worldwide are receptive to Christ than at any other time in the last 2,000 years. Even among the 36 or so countries, with a population of nearly 2 billion, who don't allow foreign missionaries, God has opened the way for a new breed of missionaries to enter in the role of Christian doctors, engineers, teachers.

Sophistication. In addition, the Church has developed unprecedented sophistication and proliferation in such methods and channels as mass media, computers, linguistics, and missionary organizations. The job ahead of us is smaller than the job behind because of those potentially effective resources.

Cooperation. Finally, there's the genuine miracle of evangelical cooperation. The Covenant developed at the Lausanne Congress on World Evangelization in 1974 has become a dynamic compass for unified action in outreach. We now have an international body capable of responding together to Christ's global cause. Fruits of this unity include cooperative research, international conferences on missionary strategy with more than 30 since 1974, publications, the sharing of resources and technology, and a growing worldwide movement of prayer. As never before we are sharing our God-given gifts in a global evangelistic partnership. For example, through international conferences, modern technology and ease of travel, God is using revived parts of His Church to teach others how to evangelize.

The implications of what's happening are staggering. What if among the over one billion Christians, God is preparing a community of conscience ready to be awakened and galvanized for biblical action on a variety of global issues?

What if awakening came to the worldwide Church so there was solidarity between Christians in the northern and southern hemispheres? What impact would that have for world evangelization among the two billion poorest of the earth? What if a thoroughly awakened Church were to ask itself: How can we work together to reach with the gospel the remaining three billion unreached of the world?

What if revival came to the 950,000 Christians already sprinkled within many unreached people-groups? Is it biblically conceivable that, prior to any new missionary penetration, these Christian minorities, freshly empowered by Christ, might accomplish far more in the advancement of the gospel than we had dreamed possible?

The Vision Within American Christianity

With 370,000 U.S. churches ministering to 144 million adults, there is currently one church for every 43 adults in our country. In most other countries, the ratio is closer to one *Christian* for every 43 adults. Are these God's beachheads, prepared to disseminate the impact of a coming wide-scale awakening?

Maybe the most significant evidence of revival at hand is the heart preparation within American evangelicalism. Dramatic preparations are evident in the growing belief that we *are* on the verge of spiritual awakening. This faith is a gift of God. Lewis Drummond has found that 85 percent of evangelicals believe this. And *Christianity Today* discovered almost 40 percent of Christian college students felt that the greatest need of the Church was for spiritual renewal. It appears that many are groping toward both local and worldwide awakening at a depth and breadth of new proportions. In 1983, a coalition on revival, with a highly acclaimed 40-person steering committee, formed to document an agenda for revival for the next decade.

Even the recently elected president of the National Council of Churches has begun his term calling for spiritual awakening in this traditionally liberal ecumenical agency. And the Sojourners Community in Washington, D.C., with all its emphasis on social justice, is gearing up for revival preaching campaigns in major cities nationwide.

Dramatic preparations for spiritual awakening throughout the worldwide Church are obvious. We sense how dramatically God seems to be setting the stage—building the fireplace—for a major new burst of heat and light. If God is preparing the Church and the world for revival, should we not expect it to be at hand? Of course, we should!

But who is ready to set the pace? Who will lead the way to the threshold? We'll find an answer in the next chapter.

6

PACESETTERS:
LEADING THE WAY TO THE
THRESHOLD

Previously, I outlined five basic theses upon which this entire book is built. The *fifth* thesis states that a movement of united prayer is normally initiated by pioneers of faith who first of all embrace God's global redemptive purpose and set the pace for serving it through concerted prayer, encouraging many others thereby to follow. Throughout biblical and church history, God has relied on a faithful few who sought Him with all their hearts and, as a result, generated spiritual surge in their generation all out of proportion to their numbers. I call these pioneers of faith "pacesetters" of a movement of prayer.

Could you be one of them?

SECRET SERVICE AGENTS
I believe God is at this very moment preparing a whole band of pacesetters to take us to the threshold. They may never be broadly organized under any particular name, such as the Evangelical Alliance in the 1800s or the Friends Missionary Prayer Band in India today, but they will nonetheless serve the Body of Christ in the most strategic way any of us could—by mobilizing concerted prayer in tune with prospects that so strongly encourage us to expect and seek spiritual awakening right now.

So, where are they? Think of them for a moment as God's

"secret service agents." For a time we may be totally unaware of who they are as they faithfully launch on in determined prayer, bearing a unique agenda—spiritual awakening—on their hearts. But eventually we will be able to pick them out—they are hard to hide, and who knows, we may even join them!

Of course, many of us are fascinated by spiritual awakening. Some are even intensely concerned. Others are willing to do whatever they can to see it come to pass—whether preaching, praying, reordering priorities, or just cleaning up their lives. But then there are those called to a ministry of intercession who set the pace for a movement of united prayer in which God intends all of us eventually to participate. Their ministry becomes God's special effort to lead us all beyond interest, concern, and good deeds into the tough-minded strategy of concerted prayer.

As a result of growth in prayer, as much as anything, these day-to-day Christians catch the fire of truth, a theology of passion, a zeal for the coming Kingdom. Increasingly they understand the glorious hope they are praying toward. They grasp fuller implications of the person and work of Christ, recognizing that two issues are involved: (1) What Christ does for us and in us (fullness) and (2) all He wants to do through His Church to establish His Kingdom throughout the earth (fulfillment).

Thus in it all, pacesetters keep us sharp on the two vivid sweeps in spiritual awakening: (1) the Lordship of Christ among His people, demonstrated as He fills His praying Church with Himself; (2) the Lordship of Christ among the nations, demonstrated through His praying Church as He fulfills His global cause.

Think of the potential! Suppose God has given enough pacesetters in the United States alone to get at least 10,000 Christians praying with them for spiritual awakening. If these 10,000 were to unite in concerts of prayer for two hours a month, that would mean 240,000 hours of united prayer for awakening each year. If those same 10,000 people also spent 10 minutes at the end of each day praying for the same issues, that would be an additional 600,000 hours a year.

If these 10,000 would be persistent to integrate the agenda of spiritual awakening into the prayer experiences they regularly share with others in the local churches and small groups to which they belong for a total of one additional hour of praying each month, that would add another 120,000 hours of prayer while encouraging many others to be on their knees to seek God's face. All of these efforts add up to almost one million additional hours of prayer for revival each year!

Of course, Scripture teaches that our Father refuses to respond to a mere piling up of our words for their own sake (Matt. 6:7-8). Still, what do you think would be the difference in the life of the Church one year from today, if it were saturated with one million hours of genuine intercession for awakening and world evangelization? And what if, in addition, that year of prayer set the pace for a large scale movement of united prayer whose momentum continues long past the first 12 months?

THE COSTS

As exciting as it all sounds, however, pacesetters will pay a price. Part of the price will be brokenness over what we see in ourselves, in our church, our nation, and our world that dishonors the name of Christ, hinders His Kingdom's advance, and robs God of His glory. As someone has said, "Revival is not organized, it is agonized," and so is a movement of prayer for revival.

It also costs a daily discipline that never ceases. To live consistently, pacesetters must develop single-minded devotion to Christ and to His global cause; they must also cultivate a vigilance in life-style to reflect all they desire and hope for.

They sometimes pay the cost of being misunderstood. Breaking with the herd mentality in order to serve the Church at this level, they may make many of us uncomfortable at first. Some of us may initially despise them even.

Jesus warned of this rejection in Matthew 10. It was one of the reactions His workers could expect when they went to harvest the fruits of the coming revival. By pulling people together in prayerful anticipation of the Kingdom they may create dissention; pacesetters will suffer rejection and even persecution. Revival seekers, by both their desperation and their hope, challenge the status quo. The call to concerted prayer even when sounded in all humility and love will end one of two ways: in decisive devotion or in decisive division.

There is also the cost of spiritual warfare. If any group of people will be opposed by the Enemy, it will be those who give themselves to prayer. No wonder Paul told the Ephesian Christians to clothe themselves with armor sufficient for a battle beyond the flesh and blood before they gave themselves to constant prayer for "all the saints" (fullness) and for "ambassadors in chains" (fulfillment) (see Eph. 6:10-20). Even the high priest Joshua, in the days of Zechariah, could not assume his priestly ministry of intercession in the Holy of Holies until Satan had been soundly rebuked and Joshua had been delivered from his adversary's false accusations (Zech. 3).

Pacesetters must be prepared for the additional cost involved as they become answers to their own prayers. They themselves may be sent by God to carry the gospel to the unreached peoples for whose sake they prayed. And that will always be costly, for any of us.

WILL YOU BE ONE?

Has God called you to be a pacesetter? Has He called you to get on the wall and set the pace for others who will climb the wall to join you, some of whom may eventually go over the wall to take the gospel to the ends of the earth? Are you willing to stand at that vantage point where you can look not only far beyond the wall to God's purposes for the whole earth but also at the crumbling ruins and marvelous potential inside the wall? And most of all, will you stand where you are able to look up and seek the face of the living God in whom lies all answers for both inside and outside the wall?

In an hour when the Church often feels as if it were up against the wall, is God calling you and me to break through that paralysis of faith? Make Isaiah's motto in 62:6-7 yours: "Take no rest, give no rest." Take no rest for yourself and give no rest to God until He has done, to the glory of His Son, everything He has promised to do. If God is calling you to be a pacesetter for a movement of prayer, you may be most concerned that if you step out in that role, you will find yourself standing alone. That was my greatest fear when I first sensed this was God's assignment for me. However, I have since discovered something wonderful through my travels here and abroad: many others are being posted on the walls. I am not alone, and neither are you.

And yet our greatest assurance that we can become persuasive pacesetters lies in our intimate link with the Chief pacesetter of prayer: the Lord Jesus. He it is who has first become the author and completer of faith for all of us (see Heb. 12:2); who has not only pioneered our way into God's presence but remains there like a high priest to represent us every time we come to the throne of grace (see Heb. 3:1; 4:14-16). He has done so at great personal sacrifice, opening the lines of communication by His cross (see Heb. 10:19-22). In essence, He is the wall on which all the watchmen stand. As He calls us to set the pace with Him in prayer (see Heb. 13:10-15) He also guarantees our success (see Heb. 13:20,21).

If you want to serve with Him as a pacesetter, then the next part of this book will be helpful to you. In it we look at principles of mobilizing, organizing, and equipping a movement of prayer for the world. The remaining chapters are written to make your work on the wall manageable and effective.

And yet, I've often found great motivation for bringing others to the threshold, as I've uncovered practical ways to get them joined in praying with me toward the vision.

What I've learned is what I now want to share.

PART II

STEPS TOWARD A MOVEMENT OF PRAYER FOR THE WORLD

7

THREE STEPS TO
GET US STARTED

Wherever you go, you will probably find three kinds of Christians: those unaware that history is happening; those who watch history happen; and those who make history happen.

In a movement of prayer for spiritual awakening, we cease to be spectators as we take initiative toward the outcome of history! Our life together presses for the fulfillment of Christ's global cause in a way nothing else can.

Let us now explore three preliminary steps which every pacesetter should take to mobilize concerted prayer for spiritual awakening.

REPENTANCE: MAKING ROOM FOR
SPIRITUAL AWAKENING

Just a few years prior to the spiritual awakenings in the New England colonies in the early 1700s, Puritan leaders in Massachusetts declared, "God hath a controversy with his New England People." They called for united repentance and prayer for a new outpouring of the Spirit. In the same attitude, delegates at the 1981 American Festival of Evangelism were given small pins made of sackcloth and ashes to wear on their dresses or lapels as an outward sign of their willingness to unite in repentance. All of this reflects the great call to revival prayer in

2 Chronicles 7:14: "If my people . . . turn from their wicked ways, and seek my face . . . . "

Repentance is the first step toward a prayer movement. It is perhaps the very best sign of a new sense of God's presence. In facing our sins we make room for deeper fellowship with Christ. Repentance reorders our lives and prepares us to encounter all that spiritual awakening will bring. Jack Miller understands: "It is simply impossible for a man to meet the Lord of glory in the full revelation of his majesty and not be grieved by his particular sins and want to confess them."[1] In realistic self-appraisal we must, as E. Stanley Jones acknowledged, "lay at his feet a self of which we are ashamed."

And yet repentance does not stop here. By a revolution of our vision for Christ, we are transformed in how we think and act and feel in our priorities and our relationships so that we might fully trust, love, and obey Him, and therefore effectively move with Him to fulfill His global cause. Thus repentance is not a negative step, it is a corrective one. By repenting in the presence of Christ we discover even more about Him and how we can serve Him.

But repent we must. How can we proclaim righteousness and truth in the gospel until we have humbled ourselves and repented of our own sins and deceptions? If we are grieving, quenching, resisting, or lying to the Spirit, we can never lay hold on the power of the Holy Spirit to be His witnesses.

The sins we confess often define what it is we are prepared to seek from God. As His light dispels some of our blindness, we want to seek even more light. The more God shows us of evil in ourselves the more we will want to intercede regarding evil wherever it is found. The more God purges us of sin, the more zealous we will be to see His whole house cleansed and become a "place of prayer for all nations" (Mark 11:15-18).

Let us explore some specific areas for confession that are critical if our repentance is to make room for spiritual awakening.

Lack of Faith

In Romans 14, Paul says that whatever is not of faith is sin. It is of the flesh. It may express itself in a lack of full enthusiasm for the things of God, in an absence of joy and praise, or in a cold heart toward the Lord Himself. The Father sent His Son into the wilderness so that He might be tested in this area of faith. Was He willing to give priority to God's Word and not to bread alone? Was He willing to give priority to God's ways and not take a shortcut to retrieve the kingdoms of earth? And, no matter what the situation, was He willing to trust God to be everything to Him that He had promised? In the same way, those who make room for spiritual awakening must cast aside, in repentance, every attitude of unbelief. We must name whatever paralyzes our faith. We must repent and believe the gospel.

We need to repent for our lack of desire for the Kingdom. We have compromised God's glory; we've been ill prepared to jealously guard it. We have been casually content with our lack of spiritual power and satisfied with mediocrity. Through Isaiah, God says to us: "These people come near to me with their mouths and honor me with their lips, but their hearts are far from me" (Isa. 29:13). And again: "A spirit of prostitution is in their hearts; they do not acknowledge the Lord. . . . When they go with their flocks and herds to seek the Lord, they will not find him; he has withdrawn himself from them" (Hos. 5:4,6).

We need to repent not so much of perversion but of indifference; not so much of pride as of preoccupation; not of failure but of frivolity; the sin we must often name is the sin of settling for second best. Not only have we lacked serious study and earnest obedience to God's Word, but we have demonstrated the shallowness of our desires by the sin of prayerlessness.

Fleshly Indulgences

According to Galatians 5, sins of the flesh cannot withstand an atmosphere of revival. Where have we indulged in lustful thoughts, or justified covetousness, or pursued material things? Where do we need to face envy and aggressive demands for our own desires and achievements to the neglect and hurt of others?

We need to become honest with our Father at every point at which we have shadowed God's glory, because we have failed to see ourselves before Christ as we really are. Our Father loves us too much to answer our prayers for spiritual awakening if, in reality, we are asking Him for help so that we can indulge in thoughts and actions of which He is unworthy (see James 4:3).

Relationships with Others

Reconciliation to one another must keep pace with all other efforts to mobilize a movement of united prayer if we are to succeed in the formation of a concerted effort and find the awakening for which we pray.

Many of us need to begin by thinking about our relationships with people in our families. Where is there lovelessness? Where have I brought shame, unworthiness, and loss of self-esteem to others? Whom have I insulted or oppressed, and whose sense of self-esteem have I lowered, or whose confidence of God's work in their lives have I retarded? Whom have I manipulated or exploited, and whom have I refused to forgive?

Spiritual Pride

We must face all the ways we use to appear more committed to Christ than we really are. Jesus' greatest wrath was aimed at the hypocrisy of spiritual leaders. God wants real people, not phonies.

Often the love of power has replaced the power of love. We can be pursuing the good in wrong ways, relying on past successes in organizations or methods—and even on ourselves—instead of the living God. As our society cries out for a response to its many needs, many of us evangelicals may be responding because we like to be at the center of attention, having others depend on us, more than because we really desire to see Christ glorified.

Some of us may also need to confess the spiritual pride we feel as specially molded instruments of God—pacesetters—for the promotion of prayer, revival, and the advancement of Christ's kingdom. Or, the pride in prayer that says "I'm thankful I'm not like others" (see Luke 18:11).

National Sins

Those involved in a movement of prayer for the world must be willing to identify with the sins of our nation and begin to lead the way in national repentance. We need to repent of the sins of

America, past and present, because we *are* Americans. Most of us need to undergo critical self-examination to determine how much of the status quo in our society we have really accepted, sometimes even with biblical rationalizations.

Look at the city or community in which you live. What sins are clearly evident to you? In what ways do you share responsibility for divorce, pornographic materials, street crimes, alcohol in the high schools, neglect of the poor? In what ways have these sins encroached on your personal life, your family's life, or your church's life?

Disobedience to the Great Commission

We must also take seriously areas of disobedience to the Great Commission. In the words of Ron Sider, we must uncover a "holy dissatisfaction with the church and society that callously tolerates widespread injustice and quietly forgets 2,000,000,000 people who have never heard of Christ."

Often we can become so occupied with the missionary endeavors in which we are involved, that we do not squarely face how much is *not* being done. The average Christian group in America does not give itself to a strategy for penetrating the kingdom of darkness in their own community, let alone to the ends of the earth. Many of us must confess that we have trouble caring about people who have never heard of Christ and who are cut off from Him by major human barriers. Some of us, who have spent hours debating what God will do with unbelieving people who die in ignorance of the gospel, need to face what God will do with disciples who have knowingly refused to move out to claim His promises in reaching the unreached. Once we do, our first option will be to repent.

And so it is critical that pacesetters lead the way in open repentance. It is we who must get this difficult and awkward ball rolling—genuinely, not for special effects—if our other efforts at mobilizing prayer are to bear fruit.

UNITY: PROVIDING WINESKINS FOR SPIRITUAL AWAKENING

Unity within the Body of Christ can provide the wineskins that capture and pour out the new wine of spiritual awakening.

Of course, in one sense, unity is the result of spiritual awakening. For example, the Evangelical Alliance, the first formal expression of broad-scale Protestant ecumenicalism, was founded in 1846 as a result of the vision developed in over a hundred years of awakenings. That experience was equally shared in Acts 2 where the entire Body of Christ on earth at that time was united as a result of the outpouring of the Holy Spirit.

Our unity with one another either verifies or denies ourselves, our church, our neighbors, our nation, and our world—our unity with Christ (see John 17). Since spiritual awakening revitalizes the whole Church, our pursuit of awakening must also demonstrate as best we can a life together that testifies to what we really believe about the Church. Are we willing to trust God for a great deal more unity and to disagree with each other about a great deal less? It is naive to think that our heavenly coach can fire up a winning team that is suited up in different uniforms and refuses to work as a team—that refuses even to huddle together just to *pray* for unity and victory!

Despite all of our diverse programs and ministries, I believe the Church in America shares much in common. While we often differ sociologically, ethnically, culturally, methodologically, and sometimes doctrinally, most Christians do not differ over the Lordship of Christ and the authority of Scripture. David Hubbard remarked to the Fourth Annual Convocation of Christian Leaders: "As Christians our fine tuning is different, but we have much more common ground than we realize." Yale church historian Kenneth Scott Latourette found that different kinds of Christianity shared a basic core of belief in Christ as Lord, the authority of Scripture, and the need to advance the gospel.

Most of us, in fact, are united in a growing desire for a deeper devotion to the Lord. Christ is at the center of our faith. Moving toward Him in prayer will naturally move us toward one another. In the *Pursuit of God,* Tozer describes how a hundred pianos, all tuned to the same fork, are automatically tuned toward each other. Is that not what a concert of prayer is all about?

Or take some of the moral concerns that most American Christians hold in common today: (1) the sanctity of human life, (2) the restoration of the family, (3) the stewardship of creation,

(4) the moral revitalization of our political processes, (5) justice for the poor, (6) freedom from nuclear holocaust, and (7) reaching the unreached. The time has also come to agree on the necessity and power of prayer if we are to see any change.

Unity within a movement of prayer also prepares new wineskins for God's mission to the world. It is tough for non-Christians to oppose a gospel that is being promulgated by a diverse coalition of godly people who, through united faith and prayer, have also become united in heart and mind with the Lord and His global cause! Such a bond will encourage us to press on beyond prayer into the work God calls us to. It will create a Church united in the battle that can be won no other way. It will provide the Lord with a strong and sturdy barn into which He may gather the wheat.

To this second step of unity all pacesetters of concerted prayer must be unswervingly committed.

DAILY DISCIPLINES: GETTING IN SHAPE FOR SPIRITUAL AWAKENING

If we really believe that God will answer our prayers for revival, then we need to prepare ourselves for the answers before they come. A concert of prayer can be as much an escape from the cause of Christ as attending a rock concert! We can busy ourselves in a cozy group that prays for the world with no real intention of getting further involved. A daily discipline that reflects what we are praying can be the antidote for this.

What Comprises a "Daily Discipline"?

Being a part of a regular concert of prayer, of course, is in itself a primary discipline that can get us in shape for a life of sacrifice. Concerted prayer becomes a microcosm involving many of the ministry dynamics needed to reach the whole world. When we seek the coming of God's Kingdom, we are living out the Kingdom by how we pray. In prayer we learn how to participate in other actions into which God will lead us.

Prayer, discipleship, and ministry work together. Prayer without discipleship and ministry can turn into a powerless pietism. But discipleship and ministry without prayer can become formal and dead. As we grow as disciples in ministry, we force ourselves to face the reality of our impotence apart from God's continued renewal in our lives. Even when we fail, it benefits us by driving us back to more determined prayer.

How Do We Get Started?

First, we must faithfully respond to all that Christ means to us now. We must be sure we are faithful to what we see of Christ now in order to be faithful to the much more we will know of Him as He answers our prayers. If the Christian life is committing all I see of myself to all I see of Christ for all I see of His global cause then when seeking His face I must give Christ my active obedience today.

Second, we must get involved in daily study of Scripture. People united in concerted prayer will be people of the Word. We need to do all we can to keep clear what it is we are praying toward. That is the key mental discipline in a movement of prayer. We must let Scripture speak to us especially about the meaning of the cross. The cross is at the heart of what we seek. It reveals the depth of our sinful condition; the love and justice of God; the ways of God and His Kingdom; the value God places on human life, including the billions who have no knowledge of His Son; and what is required of us as we seek to fulfill Christ's global cause.

Third, we need to develop a daily discipline that integrates a vision for the world into daily discipleship within the environment of united prayer. In my earlier book, *In the Gap,* I discuss initial daily disciplines needed to equip you to live like a world Christian. Among other things, I suggest a simple daily plan involving only 15 minutes a day that consists of the following disciplines:

- 5 minutes—Study what Scripture teaches on Christ's global cause. Almost 50 percent of the verses in the Bible touch on this subject.
- 4 minutes—Study other sources on world evangelization. You might read a book on evangelization, marking where you stop and picking it up there the following day.
- 3 minutes—Pray for the world, based on what you have discovered in the previous nine minutes. You literally reach out to a world of people who cannot pray for themselves.

- 2 minutes—Share with one other Christian what God has given to you in these nine minutes of "vision-building" and three minutes of prayer. This way you deposit a vision which God can use in the life of another Christian to direct him into more strategic involvement in His global cause, especially in the prospect of revival.
- 1 minute—Be still before the Lord, asking Him to speak to you any way He may choose regarding fullness and fulfillment, based on the preceding 14 minutes.

If the 10,000 pacesetters I projected earlier would discipline themselves like this for the coming revival every day for a year, it would result in another one million hours a year coupled with their one million hours of praying for revival. What impact do you think this effort would have on Christ's global cause as they continue to pray together?

There are three overriding steps a pacesetter must follow to mobilize a movement of prayer for the world: (1) repentance, (2) unity and (3) daily discipline. We are making room for spiritual awakening, joining our lives together into vessels that effectively carry His new wine of revival and getting in shape for a ministry to the world that will accelerate as God answers.

8

MOBILIZING A MOVEMENT OF PRAYER
You Can Do It!

So you want to be a pacesetter in a movement of concerted prayer for the world. Great! Past the first three steps, how do you proceed next?

PROBLEMS WITH PRAYER

Let us begin by being honest with each other. Prayer is sometimes dull, difficult, and spasmodic for everyone, including us pacesetters! Why is this? To understand the problems is to proceed with greater effectiveness in helping others on to concerted prayer.

1. We may have prayed, and prayed boldly, and not seen our prayer answered. We came away feeling that we either didn't deserve to have our prayer answered, that we failed to pray hard enough, or that maybe God simply didn't care.

2. Some of us have limited perspective of what prayer does. We suffer from historical ignorance—we never studied the topic in Scripture or in a class or in church history. Our deficiency leads us to a lack of hope. What are God's ways? What has God promised? Who does He intend to be in your life, in the life of the Church, and before the nation?

3. We each have a hidden aversion to a God who is holy and

sovereign. As fallen human beings, we in the natural seek to hide from God's presence, just as Adam did in the beginning. How often do we busy up our lives, for example, with "Christian" activities so we can excuse ourselves from getting down to business in serious prayer?

4. We may be afraid of His answers. When God answers our prayers, His decisions and actions cannot be controlled by us. Considering the impact and changes that spiritual awakening brings, do we really want it? If we are afraid of risks—of being thrust forward into new life disciplines and ministries that could change the whole course of our involvement in the world—of course we will hesitate to pray.

5. These practical problems may initially block our mobilizing efforts. But, take heart, all of them can be overcome. For remember prayer is a gift of God. A movement of concerted prayer must come from Him also. It is He, not we, who must persuade people to take up the work of prayer for awakening.

PRINCIPLES FOR MOBILIZATION

First, keep your efforts at mobilization biblical. Remember, the frontline in world evangelization is the Word of God and prayer. Scripture is the common meeting ground in our agenda for prayer for every Christian, no matter what pool of renewal or denomination they come from.

Second, set the pace in prayer yourself, even if initially no one else joins you. Remember Zechariah 8:20-21? Those who call others to prayer conclude their invitation with the words, "I myself am going."

Third, as you seek to mobilize others, be humble. Standing at the threshold knocking does not make me any more spiritual than those who have yet to join me.

Fourth, integrate the agenda of spiritual awakening into every other prayer situation. Do this, for instance, when you are called on to pray during your weekly small-group Bible study. The more you integrate, the more you alert others to your concerted prayer vision, and to the good reasons to get involved.

Fifth, begin with the few. Don't be dismayed if that is all there is for a while. God is already raising up people of prayer long before you begin to mobilize them. Where will you find these few? Let me suggest two prime candidates: (1) those who are seeking after Christ, who want a deeper reality in their walk with Him; (2) those who have a sense of mandate to redirect their lives for maximum ministry to the world.

Sixth, seek the seekers. How can you do this effectively? You could begin by widely circulating an invitation for others to join those of you who have begun, and see who turns up.

Seventh, be enthusiastic. People need to know that you really believe in what you're doing. But don't force the issue too far, because there is a time when people are ready to seek, and a time when they are not.

Eighth, listen for barriers to prayer. Are people afraid of what it will cost them? Have they had bad experiences? Is their vision fuzzy about what they are praying toward? Are they struggling to integrate the issues of spiritual awakening into their problems of daily life? Is it possible that there is sin in their lives that prevents them from drawing near to God? Are there broken relationships with other Christians that have soured them on Kingdom concerns?

Ninth, as you begin to understand these barriers, it is important to help people see that their involvement can meet their felt needs. Most of us approach any new challenges on the basis of "what's in it for me?" Help people to see that concerted prayer is compatible to who they are, relevant to what they need, and desirable in achieving God's life objectives for them.

Tenth, fire imaginations with the biblical and historical patterns of spiritual awakening, and with evidence that God is preparing for another such work today. Give them a new vision of the Church, a new vision of God's work among the nations, a new vision of hope about the future and the advancement of God's Kingdom.

Eleventh, show people that concerts of prayer are manageable. Maybe your concert will be two hours one evening a month, 20 minutes once a week after each worship service, or 15 minutes after each campus fellowship meeting. Show people that the concert won't demand an unreasonable amount of time. Even 15 minutes, if clearly on target, can be a concert of prayer.

Twelfth, once you get them there, get them into the action. Have different individuals lead various components of the meeting, do research on information to be prayed about, recruit others, or send out a little newsletter to all regular participants.

Thirteenth, use this book to help you mobilize and train others. You might do so by having them read through it at a chapter a week. Or, you may want to form a small group to study the book together prior to incorporating newcomers into the ongoing concert of prayer. To help you, a seven-session, small group study guide is found in the back of this book.

Fourteenth, tap into the growing network of other united prayer efforts. The National Prayer Committee can help you do this.[1] We need to hear what God is doing in the variety of corporate prayer expressions, and we need to communicate with each other about what we are learning from God about revival prayer, about concerted prayer, about mobilizing prayer, and about answers to our prayers. Those who have studied previous awakenings note that one critical human contribution to expanding prayer movements was clear, accurate, sufficient communication between those who prayed.

Fifteenth, expect a battle. When it comes don't let it throw you. Satan's greatest concern, next to preventing the gospel from reaching those who haven't heard, is to sabotage prayer movements that call for God to revive His Church and advance His Kingdom. He will try to discourage you, whether it be by interruptions as you pray together, by dwindling numbers, or by those who misunderstand and even question your efforts at prayer with, say, charges of spiritual elitism. The battle is sure to become toughest as your prayer group increasingly experiences the hand-to-hand cosmic warfare described in Daniel 9 and 10, Ephesians 6, and Revelation 12. Concerts of prayer are serious business.

USE OF A COVENANT

In a covenant, a group of people affirm that God has called them together for a specific purpose. A covenant states the intention of, and gives identity to, those who are prepared to be faithful to that calling. It also states the prayer movement's focus and its expectations. It forges us together in a sense of common mission.

You may want to include in it statements regarding: (1) the

shape of the concert itself; (2) the intention of its members to participate regularly; (3) their intention to carry the issues with them back to their own daily prayer life; (4) the willingness of concert participants to integrate the agenda for spiritual awakening into all other times of prayer with Christians; (5) your intention to seek those whom God may be preparing to be a part of your prayer concert.

POSSIBLE PITFALLS

The path to every worthwhile endeavor is filled with pitfalls; mobilizing a prayer movement is no exception. I can name at least three pitfalls you should beware of.

First, avoid a naive optimism that expects immediate response on the part of everyone you invite to join. Keep your eyes fixed on Christ rather than on immediate circumstances or human enthusiasm.

Second, never forget that you are a servant who is helping fellow Christians become all they are meant to be. In your fervor to make things happen, be sure you do not come across to your friends as prideful, self-righteous, a know-it-all, or disrespectful of what God has already done for them.

Third, we who mobilize prayer in a "Christian" country like America must always remember that our priority in prayer is for a new demonstration of the Lordship of Christ in His Church. It is not for the theocratization of our society at large. It is for spiritual awakening rather than cultural renaissance though that may come. It is for the fulfillment of the Great Commission rather than the rallying of forces around patriotic ideals. The pressure will be there for us Americans to allow our prayer movement to slide away from the Kingdom's agenda and toward a civil/religious exercise for endorsing fuzzy forms of moral renewal. Of course, Kingdom prayers on behalf of our nation are always welcome—and can result in moral renewal.

A CONSULTATION ON CONCERTS OF PRAYER

If you are mobilizing prayer in a community-wide or campus-wide effort, you may need to hold a one-time consultation with church or campus leaders. You will want to determine together what steps to take to get praying people united. Such a consultation can help to insure that what we do is truly a cooperative effort.

In the back of this book is a suggested outline for such a one-day meeting of leaders and a set of proposals for discussion.

FORMING A STEERING COMMITTEE

It's easier to steer a bike once its moving. But unless some steering goes on after you have started, an accident is inevitable.

History shows that in most revivals there have been aberrations as one group or another has veered away into a variety of sub-biblical tangents. This could happen to your movement of prayer for revival. So, once it is underway, part of your responsibility in mobilizing it is to steer it on course. Do not try this alone. Form a steering committee.

That steering committee may initially consist of the original three or four who joined you when your concert of prayer began. Or, it may consist of leaders on your campus or in your community who, as a result of a consultation, expressed a strong commitment to the concert of prayer idea.

What are the responsibilities of the steering committee?

First, be faithful in attending. Every other responsibility will be impossible to carry out unless the committee is regularly involved. You are setting an example as well.

Second, the steering committee should meet between concerts of prayer—unless the concerts are held frequently—to evaluate what's happening and to take corrective action when necessary.

	FULLNESS			FULFILLMENT		
REJOICE	global issues		local issues	global issues		local issues
REPENT	global issues		local issues	global issues		local issues
REQUEST	global issues		local issues	global issues		local issues

Some steering committees have found it very helpful to use the grid in diagram 1 for analyzing each prayer meeting to determine if a good balance was maintained. In chapter 9 we will discuss in more detail how to use this helpful tool.

At times your steering committee may want to involve other members of your concert in a brief time of evaluation. Encourage others to participate as much as possible in vision, planning, and evaluating the prayer movement.

Third, the committee should pray for concert participants. God acts as a result of your prayers, and His work while you meet in prayer is as basic as what He does after you meet. As we enter new dimensions of spiritual aggression, we must keep the concert before the Lord, asking Him to lead it by His direction, organization, and agenda, and to protect it against all the attacks of the evil one. The steering committee also should pray that the other pray-ers will not become discouraged and that God will keep them faithful to what He has called them to do.

It may seem strange to have a prayer meeting to pray for a prayer meeting; after all, who will then pray for the prayer meeting that prays for the prayer meeting, ad infinitum? Of course, the ultimate one praying for all pray-ers is the one who ever lives to make intercession for us (Heb. 7:25). Still, I know your steering committee will not regret the time it spends praying for the concerts of prayer.

Fourth, the steering committee should facilitate communication between meetings. Communicating with participants is especially important if your concert meets no more often than once a month. A letter in which the committee makes suggestions for sharpening the prayer movement or highlights guidelines for the next concert of prayer is helpful. The letter can also keep participants updated on issues that need to be addressed in prayer and to report to them on fast-breaking answers.

Fifth and finally, the steering committee should give primary leadership in coordinating the concerts of prayer. By their model and their exhortations, the leaders set the atmosphere from the very start of the meeting.

Others have done this successfully. In God's time, so can you!

ORGANIZING A CONCERT OF PRAYER
Of Course You Can!

There you are in your venue—a large living room, a lounge on campus or a church sanctuary. Before you, 25 eager people sit ready to be joined in revival prayer. You and three or four others have been praying for this moment for months. The clock strikes 7:00 P.M. as one more person slips through the back door. It is time to begin your first concert of prayer.

Now what? Despite your best recruitment efforts, unless you know how to organize and lead the meeting it will probably end up like a lot of other prayer meetings—a lot of talk about prayer but little prayer! Or worse yet, just plain boring.

Don't despair! You can lead an exciting concert of prayer!

WELCOME TO A REAL, LIVE CONCERT OF PRAYER!

The information in this chapter can help you lead a two-hour concert of prayer. The practical format suggested has been developed experimentally in a variety of situations and with many groups around the world over the past six years.

Our format really *does* work! It creates a satisfying prayer experience, even when groups from diverse backgrounds gather together. It keeps people on target, giving them a sense of strategic impact for the Kingdom. And it is transferable by those who have done it, so that concerts of prayer can multiply. The format works effectively, whether with a band of five or a company of 500!

Distinctives That Shape the Format

But first, let's uncover the reasons for this particular format and approach. "Concerts of Prayer" is a term used widely to define a distinctive prayer gathering, differing at a number of points from most other times Christians pray together. The distinctives suggest a different approach to how the prayer meeting is shaped and led. Here are 10 distinctives, each of which comes into play in the practical format that follows. Understanding these distinctives will help you use the format with greater confidence.

1. A concert of prayer is marked by a spirit of celebration. Throughout we rejoice in hope (Rom. 5:1-5), anticipating all God has promised to us in answer to our prayers for spiritual awakening and world evangelization.

2. A concert of prayer incorporates a broad scope of prayer concerns. Yet our focus is on two major Kingdom themes (like the treble and bass clefs of a music score): *fullness* (revival or awakening in the Church) and *fulfillment* (the advancements of God's Kingdom in the world). The Lord's Prayer models both of these key concerns (Matt. 6:9-13).

3. A concert of prayer provides a visible expression of the unity in the Body of Christ. Like the variety of instruments in an orchestra, brought together under one Conductor (Jesus Christ) to play from one Score (the Scriptures), so believers united in prayer can release the music of God's Kingdom purposes for the whole world to hear. In a concert of prayer, Christians can experience at deep levels the unity Jesus intended (John 17). Through corporate intercession we are newly forged to Christ, to each other and to Christ's mission in the world. While we may not yet be able to achieve visible unity in other areas, certainly we can and must do so in the arena of biblically-grounded prayer, especially prayer for awakening and evangelization.

4. A concert of prayer provides a way to network the Body of Christ within a city or on a campus. It helps us find one another across barriers, differences, spheres of influence and ministries that otherwise often divide us. It provides a neutral

meeting ground. Here, despite our differences, the overarching Kingdom concerns that touch all of us can become our shared focus through united praying and, as a result, through joint-ministries (Rom. 12:1-5, 11-13).

5. A concert of prayer draws together and benefits Christians from all different spheres. The explanation is simple. When God answers Kingdom-sized prayers offered to Him unitedly, everyone in the prayer movement, plus the fellowships they represent, share together in being blessed (awakening) and in becoming a blessing to the families of the earth (world evangelization). God's whole vision for the whole city or campus and, ultimately, beyond must be realized through the whole Body. Thus, His answers are for the whole Body, too. A local concert of prayer may be the one ongoing effort among believers that forgoes any reasons for competition (see 1 Tim. 2:1-8).

6. A concert of prayer provides a point of contact for praying people and prayer groups within a city or on a campus. Here they can periodically interface, help each other expand their Kingdom concerns in prayer, sharpen one another's prayer ministry within the fellowships from which they come and take new faith and vision back into their ongoing prayer efforts day by day. Prayer leaders and prayer groups will come from at least three major parts of the Body: the church sphere, the mission sphere and the youth sphere. All three should be represented in a concert. Those from the church sphere bring strong nurturing concerns which relate to revival; those from the mission sphere bring concerns for outreach and advancement; those from the youth sphere often carry fresh dreams and aspirations, as well as new leadership potential, for nurture and outreach ministries. We all need one another.

7. A concert of prayer offers a training ground for mobilizing prayer throughout the Body of Christ. Through its regular impact on those who gather to pray, it naturally accelerates prayer and sharpens our prayer agenda in all efforts in prayer everywhere within God's family. To help insure its contribution as a training ground, concerts should be sufficiently organized so that participants can adapt what they gain from the experience back into the situations where they pray with others the rest of the month. Thus, a concert of prayer is both a workshop on

prayer and a ministry of prayer (see Luke 11:1). Along with the answers it secures from God's hand for the Church and the world, this training is another way prayer movements act as God's servants in the work of His Kingdom.

8. A concert of prayer provides a sustaining foundation for ministry both to the city or campus and among the nations. It is a base of operations for advancing Christ's global cause as it: (a) equips the pray-ers to become more spiritually attuned servants; (b) helps the pray-ers to rededicate themselves to be Christ's ambassadors in any way He chooses; (c) plants ministry to earth's unloved and unreached; (d) attempts, at times, to link up consciously the prayer movement with specific outreach efforts (evangelistic, justice, church-planting, etc.); (e) prepares the way for all other ministries inside and outside the Church as God goes ahead of us by actually answering our cries for spiritual awakening and world evangelization (see Ps. 65:1-8; Acts 13:1-4).

9. A concert of prayer historically has retained a sense of manageability, both in format and in frequency. Often in the past these concerts have met once a month, allowing busy Christians to rearrange their schedules so that united prayer gets the priority it deserves. That way, those who participate, coming from different fellowships with differing responsibilities to those bodies, can still find a common time to gather without jeopardizing their other commitments. The same sensitivity is in evidence in prayer movements today.

10. A concert of prayer is part of a movement, not just an event. It is part of a process in which we are moving on from where things are (in us, in the Church, in the world) to where God desires and deserves things to be. We are involved in a long-term ministry, seeking long-term impact for the Kingdom through united prayer. This requires that those who join in be persevering servants, consistently involved on a regular basis and actively inviting others to join with them month by month (see Acts 1:14; 2:1, 42; 4:23-24).

Planning + Variety = A Creative Format

Though this chapter presents ideas that you and your steering committee can implement, you will find more suggestions than you can handle all at once. There are many creative ways a concert of prayer can establish a format that includes the freedom and active discipline that will allow the Holy Spirit to pray through the whole group. Our suggested format provides a basic structure that reflects important principles, yet with enough variety to give color and music to the format. After all, you are leading a concert of prayer!

Planning

• Determine where you will meet. I suggest you secure a location that is central to your community or campus. You may want to move the concert from church to church. If you seek to interface lay people with students, try a concert of prayer on the campus in your community, thus allowing the students to host the prayer meeting.

• Maintain a regular and convenient schedule. All of us suffer from overscheduling, hyperactivity and too many demands. It is important that your concert meet on the same day and hour every time, to avoid confusion.

• Assign a leader to guide each concert.

Variety

• Encourage variations of posture during the meeting. Tell people they're free to pray sitting, kneeling, standing, walking, or even flat on their faces.

• Encourage variation in the length of prayers. Assure people that prayers of one sentence are fine. So are prayers of one or two minutes as long as the prayer comes from the heart and is in keeping with the Word of God.

• Vary how group prayer is directed. At times a leader may call out, "Let's just have a time of rejoicing" or "Will someone lead us in prayers of repentance regarding the sins of the Church." Or you may be very practical: "For the next few minutes as we pray fullness prayers, let's name specific churches where we would like to see God work" or "As we pray for a little while on fulfillment issues, feel free to state both the name of your own neighbors and people groups far away among whom you would like to see the gospel at work."

NOW, LET'S LOOK AT THE FORMAT

The suggested format is *only one model,* but it does reflect many of the important distinctives that must be retained in concerts of prayer.

Variety in format is important. So don't let the arbitrary time allotments feel overly restrictive for you. On the one hand, order and timing are important, to insure a balanced, in-depth coverage of the issues for which the movement exists. Further, some structure and control is required to insure a meaningful experience for the pray-ers, especially since they come from many backgrounds and meet only periodically like this.

But we must also remain open to the Spirit's direction. Ultimately, Jesus, not our humanly devised format, conducts each concert! Freedom and improvisation do have a place in God's Kingdom symphonies. So while we pursue orderliness, at the same time we keep our eyes on the Conductor, our Lord Jesus, for any adjustments He may want to make.

One nice feature of this particular format is that its basic components could be covered more briefly in a 30-minute gathering, or they can be expanded past two hours in order to provide a half-night of prayer. So, in the end, timing is up to the local prayer leaders, under the Spirit's guidance. But many find that at least two hours are needed to give people a satisfying prayer experience. And people usually can't believe how swiftly two hours can pass in a prayer event of this nature!

Now, let's discuss the components in the format. Each component appears for a purpose. Experience has shown each to be essential in order to insure good coverage of the strategic issues for which the concert exists. Therefore, please stress to the pray-ers that they keep their thoughts and prayers relative to each component as you move through it. For example, urge that during the Fullness segment, intercession should focus primarily on issues relating to awakening in the Church, while prayer for world needs can come later in the Fulfillment segment.

But encourage everyone to work at maintaining a proper blend of rejoicing, repenting and requesting within segments, though the celebration component will be mostly rejoicing. Of course, the primary response experienced throughout all concerts is this: seeking God's glory and Kingdom in Jesus Christ.

One final insight: The format can help you put people at ease. Coming from different backgrounds as we do, the format permits us to vary in our perspectives and ways of expressing ourselves in prayer, so as to make uniquely meaningful contributions to the whole concert thrust. Encourage everyone, however, to work at being sensitive to one another—neither offending nor judging one another—as we seek to pray in "harmony" and with singleness of purpose. Remind people to listen to one another, building our prayers on one another, and learn from one another about how and what to pray.

SUGGESTED FORMAT FOR A CONCERT OF PRAYER

Following the pattern of concerts of prayer over the past 250 years, as well as prayer movements emerging nationwide and worldwide today, here is one model of a format for a two-hour concert of prayer. The approach provides not only a satisfying experience during a prayer concert, but can be adapted back in the churches, fellowships and ministries from which we come, so that the vision and ministry of united prayer may spread.

Here are the basic components for a concert of prayer:
- Celebration
- Seeking for Fullness
- Testimonies
- Preparation
- Seeking for Fulfillment
- Grand Finale
- Dedication

CELEBRATION (15 min.)
- Praise in hymns and choruses, focused on awakening and mission
- Reports of God's answers to prayers offered up during previous concerts
- Prayers of praise for God's faithfulness, for His Kingdom, for His Son

PREPARATION (20 min.)
- Welcome to the concert!
- Overview: Why are we here?
- Biblical perspectives on what we're praying (toward awakening, mission)
- Preview of the format

- Teaming-up in partners and in huddles

DEDICATION (5 min.)
- Commitment: to be servants through prayer and to be used in answer to our prayers
- Thanksgiving: for the privilege of united prayer and for those with whom we unite
- Invitation for Christ to lead the concert and to pray through us
- Hymn of praise

SEEKING FOR FULLNESS/AWAKENING IN THE CHURCH (30 min.)
- In partners—for personal revival
- In huddles—for awakening in our local churches and ministries
- As a whole—for awakening in the Church worldwide
- Pause to listen to our Father
- Chorus

SEEKING FOR FULFILLMENT/MISSION AMONG THE NATIONS (30 min.)
- In partners—for personal ministries
- In huddles—for outreach and mission in our city or campus
- As a whole—for world evangelization
- Pause to listen to our Father
- Chorus

TESTIMONIES: WHAT HAS GOD SAID TO US HERE? (10 min.)
- On Fullness (awakening)
- On Fulfillment (mission)

GRAND FINALE (10 min.)
- Offering ourselves to be answers to our prayers and also to live accordingly
- Prayer for God's empowerment in our own lives for ministry
- Prayer for prayer movements locally and worldwide
- Offering praise to the Father who will answer our concert of prayer

- Leave to watch and serve "in concert"

GUIDELINES ON COMPONENTS AND ACTION STEPS

- **Celebration** (15 min.)

Be sure that praise focuses on God's character and ways in Christ. Use this time as well to highlight important issues in spiritual awakening and world evangelization.

Provide a good mixture of hymns and choruses, making sure to tie each song into the major themes of concerts of prayer. This can be done by just a few brief comments (no preaching allowed!) to introduce each new number. In between songs, you may want to have a few brief reports on how God has already been answering your previous concerts, either in new expressions of revival (locally or worldwide) or new advances of the Kingdom (locally or worldwide).

Toward the end of this component, have three or four lead the entire group in brief prayers of praise for all you've sung and heard.

- **Preparation** (20 min.)

First, welcome everyone to the concert. If at a host church, the host pastor may want to do this. Then, explain the purpose and distinctives of a concert of prayer, restating exactly why we're here (1-2 min.).

Next, turn to the Scriptures to provide a brief biblical perspective on what God wants us to pray toward as we seek spiritual awakening and world evangelization (10 min.). In other words, what is the hope the Scriptures set before us that needs to form our prayer agenda? Books like Isaiah and Ephesians provide a wealth of such studies.

Then introduce everyone to the basic components of the format, to acquaint them with the approach to the rest of the meeting. You may want to have it printed out and in their hands. Explain the flow of the concert, why each component is important and how each fits with the others. It is at this point that you may want to make a few suggestions, such as being sensitive to each other in how long our prayers are or how loud and so on. You may also have a handout highlighting five or so key issues under Fullness and Fulfillment to be prayed over during this concert of prayer.

Next, help people know one another. Find out who is at the concert for the first time by a show of hands. Give them a card to fill out their address and their church or fellowship. Also have people identify the churches, groups or fellowships that they represent, to give everyone a sense of how God is bringing the whole Body together. Have one representative from each body call out its name, possibly.

Finally, have them form partners—maybe with a shy friend or with a new friend. Give them 30 seconds to get acquainted. Then, form huddles by putting together three sets of partners (six people to a huddle). Allow another 30 seconds to get acquainted. You might observe for everyone that throughout the evening they will pray in partners for each other's needs for revival and in ministry, in huddles for the needs of Christians and the unreached locally, and as a total group for the needs of Christians and the unreached worldwide. Someone has called these the duets, ensembles and symphonies in your concert of prayer!

- **Dedication** (5 min.)

One person on your leadership team now steps forward to lead the whole group through a period of guided, silent prayer. After each suggestion is made, give them a time of quiet to make it a personal point of prayer. Then close that period with a brief prayer from the leader.

First, suggest that they reaffirm their desire to scrve the Church and world through this ministry of intercession. Have them reaffirm, as well, their readiness to be used of God in answer to any prayers agreed on in the concert.

Next, lead them in a period of confession of any known sin, so that they might be clean and ready to pray. Then have them personally ask and receive the Spirit's filling in their lives so that He might lead them in all that they pray.

Now, guide them to quietly thank God for everyone else gathered into the concert of prayer, and have them ask God to blend all of them together so that they really do become a great symphony of rejoicing, repentance and requesting throughout the meeting.

Finally, the leader should offer an audible prayer on behalf of everyone, inviting the Lord Jesus to take up His role as High Priest among those present and to bring all together into His ministry of prayer for fullness and fulfillment. Ask Him to make the concert His prayer meeting from beginning to end.

He or she might conclude the audible prayer by having the pray-ers join in a chorus that focuses specifically on Christ and His Kingdom.

• Seeking for Fullness/Awakening to Christ Within the Church (30 min.)

In united prayer, guided by another member of the leadership team, your concert begins to concentrate on seeking the fullness of Christ in the life of the Church, both locally and worldwide. "Fullness" is a popular word used to describe revival or awakening (see Eph. 1:21-23, *NIV*).

First, have them pray in partners. Have them turn immediately to one another and take 30 seconds apiece to share where they need personal revival and renewal, then begin praying for awakening and renewal in each other's lives. Prayers should be brief, about one minute apiece. Each may pray for their partner what they also desire of revival in their own lives as well.

After about 3 or 4 minutes, call for the huddles to form immediately, as partners quickly put their heads together with other partners. Urge them to pray for awakening in their own fellowships and in the Body of Christ throughout their city or on their campus. Ask that prayers be brief, based on Scripture and specific to the needs of the situation. Huddles may continue for approximately 7 minutes.

Then, call the huddles back together so as to pray as a whole. Ask for a few to lead the entire prayer meeting in specific concerns for spiritual awakening worldwide—either for the Church in other parts of the world or for the Church generally according to its needs in this generation. Be sure to encourage people to speak up as they pray in the large group. As a leader, you may want to give some designated points for prayer now and then, asking for someone to lead all present in prayer for one specific issue or matter (see suggestions in chapter 10. Pray as a whole for 15 minutes.

You might conclude this segment in creative ways, such as having pastors and other spiritual leaders, like campus staff workers with local student ministries, stand to receive special prayer for their ministry to the Body of Christ. You may want to ask a few nearby them to stand and lay their hands on them where they are.

Finally, lead the whole group into a period of listening (2 min.). Ask for complete silence. Ask each one to see if God has something He may want to say to them personally about issues touching His concerns for spiritual awakening—either in them, in local fellowships or in the Church-at-large. What God says to them will form some of the testimonies at the end of the Concert.

Conclude the listening by leading everyone in a chorus or song that focuses on spiritual awakening (1 min.). Be sure to let them stand.

Note: Have a piano or a guitar play a quiet chorus between partners and huddles and between huddles and large group to help bring people out of prayer and to attention.

• Seeking for Fulfillment/Sharing in Christ's Mission Among the Nations (30 min.)

In united prayer, another leader begins to help your group concentrate on seeking the fulfillment of Christ's global cause among those who do not belong to His Kingdom, both locally and worldwide.

"Fulfillment" is a popular word used to describe mission, outreach and world evangelization in all its many facets (see Eph. 1:2-11, *NIV*). The special focus should be on the 3 billion currently beyond the reach of the gospel. But you should also touch on issues of hunger, justice, governments, poverty, war, disease, immorality and so on, all of which are part of the battle with the kingdom of darkness.

The segments are the same as before—partners, huddles, as a whole—and listening with the same time frames. But this time partners pray for each other's ministry for Christ in the world. Huddles pray for new advancements of the Kingdom in their city or on their campus. Finally, the whole group is led by a few to pray for the work of the gospel all over the world. Again, the up-front leader may want to suggest some specific key issues that need special attention. See chapter 10 for a list of a few important issues.

You might conclude the large group prayer time in creative ways, such as asking missionaries, those preparing for missionary work or those involved in exceptionally difficult ministry to locally unreached people to stand for special prayer, as we did earlier with spiritual leaders in the Church.

During the two minutes of complete silence, ask each one to listen to God to see if he has something He may want to say to them personally about issues touching His concerns for world evangelization—on their campus, in their city or around the globe.

Conclude the listening by leading everyone in a chorus or song that focuses on world evangelization. Have them stand to sing.

• Testimonies: What Has God Said to Us? (10 min.)

This component provides an opportunity for the pray-ers to find out how God has already begun to answer their prayers during the concert. Already He is working in them as they have prayed and listened. Possibly, He has shared insights or dreams that will benefit the whole group. These need to be heard.

First, ask for a few testimonies on fullness. That is, what has God said to some; what has He opened up to them that should be shared for the sake of the whole group? It might be a Scripture verse. It might be an exhortation on an issue that needs specific prayer in our daily quiet times. It might be new insights on awakening or an expanded understanding of what God is preparing to do in awakening. It might be a word of repentance or of hope. The key is to keep the testimonies short, to the point and for the encouragement of the whole group.

Next, ask for a few testimonies on fulfillment. That is, what has God said to some regarding the advancement of His Kingdom that should be shared for the sake of the whole group? Again a variety of things should be shared. It might be a new dream or vision for ministry to which others will rally. In fact, this opportunity to share a vision for some area of outreach can become, over time, a wonderful way to insure that our "waiting" on God gets translated into action together. Or it might involve a new sense of a personal incentive in an area of existing ministry. This will encourage others to renewed commitment in ministry. It might also be a Scripture verse or an exhortation toward courage or compassion.

Note: Emphasize that the sharing must be related to what God has done or said during the concert itself. This isn't a time for general sharing.

Throughout, the sharing needs to be done for the encouragement of the whole group and not just for allowing individuals to talk about themselves. The bottom line of all testimonies is to hear from God and to recognize how fully He has bee involved with us throughout the concert of prayer.

- **Grand Finale** (10 min.)

Have everyone move into a time of personal, private prayer. At this point each pray-er offers his or her life to be used in any way God may choose, in answer to the prayers agreed on in the concert. They also ask His help in living lives daily that are increasingly more consistent with what they have prayed at the concert. This two-minute offering may be even more meaningful if those who can do so get down on their kneeds, as an outward demonstration of commitment. For variety, they may even be encouraged to pray audibly and simultaneously, as Christians do in many parts of the world.

Then, moving back into huddles, ask one person in each huddle to pray that God would begin in them the work of awakening and of bringing forth new ministries to the world. Pray as well for the power of the Holy Spirit in it all. In other words, have the huddles "personalize" the vision and the thrust of the entire concert (2 min.).

For the next three minutes, ask the concert to stand to form again as one body, while three people from the leadership team lead in prayer for a growing prayer movement for fullness and fulfillment. For example, have one person pray that God will daily keep all of you consistent in prayer. Have someone else pray for the emerging prayer movement in your city or on your campus. Have a third pray for God to raise up concerted prayer in the church worldwide.

Finally, conclude the concert of prayer by offering prayers of praise (3-4 leading) in anticipation of the answers coming out of your united intercession. These prayers are followed with a final hymn of celebration focusing on Christ and His Kingdom.

Urge people to greet one another as they leave. Encourage them to continue to reflect on and pray for the issues on which the concert focused. And provide them with a flyer giving details on the next concert of prayer.

Further Helps: If you have difficulties using this format in leading others, here are four suggestions: (1) Attend a concert near you, and learn as you observe others using it. (2) Make some adjustments in the format so that if fits you and your group while still keeping the basic components (3) Write to InterVarsity Christian Fellowship, c/o "Concerts of Prayer Project" (6400 Schroeder Rd., P.O. Box 7895, Madison, Wisconsin 53707-7895) for a detailed handbook. (4) Other helps are also available from InterVarsity, including a video training series on concerts of prayer.

CONCERT OF PRAYER ESSENTIALS

No matter what format you follow, it is helpful for your concert to maintain the following elements somewhere during the meeting:

- Praise God in song and prayer.
- Invite Christ to be the "conductor" of the meeting.
- Confess and pray for cleansing.
- Tell "why we are here."
- Teach a brief Bible lesson regarding fullness and fulfillment.
- Report on what God has done in the past or is doing today in response to movements of prayer.
- Ask for testimonies from those whose lives are being transformed by their involvement in the concerts.
- Review specific guidelines the steering committee feels would help keep the concert on target.
- Review some specific issues that help make up the agenda of fullness and fulfillment.
- Spend an extended time of prayer for fullness and fulfillment.
- End with a word of promise from Scripture on how God answers prayer.

- Record the prayers that have been offered so you can watch for the answers.
- Suggest a Scripture passage for each participant to meditate on in preparation for the next concert.

MORE GUIDELINES

Some of the following will be more relevant in the early days of your concert, some later on. At times it might be good to publish pertinent guidelines and send them to participants between prayer meetings.

- Remind participants to enter the room quietly.
- Encourage them to think of themselves not only as a family in prayer, but as a team involved in a ministry of prayer.
- Define the concert of prayer as both a school of prayer and a ministry of prayer: a time to learn as well as a time to give.
- Remind them that concerts of prayer are a distinctive type of prayer meeting. A concert of prayer is a ministry of intercession, a ministry to the Church and to the world with a specific target: spiritual awakening—fullness and fulfillment issues.
- I recommend placing a map where it is visible to everyone. During prayer, someone may wish to look up and scan the world map to recall an issue they need to address.
- Encourage people not to feel self-conscious. Remind them that any prayer they make—made according to the Word of God, from a heart of faith and in Jesus' name—is acceptable to Him.
- Encourage sensitivity to varieties of praying. You may have Pentecostals and non-Pentecostals, educated and less educated, rich and poor, young and old, etc. Ask participants to accept one another's prayer styles.
- Suggest that people listen carefully to one another's prayers, seeking not only to express agreement when appropriate but also to look for ways to build on one another's prayers. Sometimes a whole series of prayers may build one on the other around a specific topic until that area is covered by the group.
- Remind participants about the length of their prayers. They are praying in a group, so they should think of others and not just of themselves in what they choose to pray about and how they construct their prayers.

- Don't hesitate to praise God at points along the way. Try to do so within the context of the reason for concerts: the grand sweeps of concern for fullness and fulfillment.
- There are three paces of intercession: solidarity, advocacy, and pursuit. Acknowledge these paces and encourage people to develop their prayers along all three lines.
- Give guidelines on times of silence. Silence can be very significant. At times, God may call us to be quiet enough before Him that we might hear all He is asking us to do. There are many things a concert of prayer can pray about but there may be only a few things it should pray about on any specific occasion. During times of silence, you not only have opportunity to review what has already been prayed, but you can ask God to lead you even more clearly about what you must pray before the concert is over.
- Encourage asking God questions and then pausing to listen. Many of the psalms appear to be this type of praying. It may be appropriate for someone to lead out in prayer with a series of questions, each followed by a few moments of silence.
- Singing may be appropriate at times in order to strengthen the faith and vision of the group for the ministry of intercession and to get our eyes more firmly back on Christ and His purposes. Again, it is important that all singing fit the specific agenda and purpose of concerts.
- Confession is an important part of intercession. Sometimes the confessions may be for individual lives, sometimes for local churches or the Church worldwide; at other times they may need to confess the sins of our nation and of our world. They may need to confess lovelessness, unbelief, disobedience or cry out to God in repentance for their ineffective impact with the gospel. In all confession, participants must be sure that the burden is not primarily for themselves—their sins, their helplessness, their needs—but is for the whole Church, beginning with the church where they live. In all confession, the concert must continue to move away from the problems and look away to the person of Christ, in whom there is forgiveness.
- Publish a statement of faith broad enough to allow any genuine Christian to participate, but clear enough to ensure that pray-

ing does not end up on a doctrinal tangent. I recommend the *Lausanne Covenant on World Evangelization,* a widely used statement. A copy may be obtained by writing to C.W.E., Whitefield House, 186 Kennington Park Rd., London SE11 4BT, England.

- Encourage people to think about their prayers before they begin, using the grid if necessary.

- Encourage people to pray frequently about those things God has led them to pray for since the last concert.

- As you pray, encourage participants to use Scripture in forming the requests they make. Encourage people to open their Bibles during the time of prayer and to actually turn to passages and pray them back to the Lord in their own words.

- Reassure people that there is nothing wrong with moving from general issues to more specific ones. Most of the prayers of Scripture are prayers formed in generalities though for specific situations or people.

- Remind people that even when they pray for "local concerns"—either for themselves or their church or their city—they need to be encouraged to examine the global implications of God's answers to those prayers, and to say so to Him.

- Remind them to avoid the "privatization" of their requests. It is possible to pray about fullness and me or fulfillment and me and never get down to praying for fullness and fulfillment as it relates to the Lord and His global cause.

- Remind them that they are holding one another accountable in their daily prayer lives, as well as in their daily disciplines, to be living out what they pray together in concert.

- Encourage faithfulness in attending the concerts of prayer. Remember, it may be months or years before all prayers are answered. Periodically, review your covenant if you form one.

- Remind people to keep a balance between the real and ideal as they evaluate the meetings. The real is never what we want it to be, but most of our ideals are usually unattainable. Without this balance, participants might give up and withdraw from the concerts or try to place the blame on others or go off and start their own groups. Welcome feedback to the steering committee if participants have ways to strengthen the concerts.

- Encourage members of the concert to be responsible for research on specific prayer issues, such as needs of our society, missions concerns, or specific people groups to be reached. This way, they will be better equipped to give intelligent leadership in prayer during the next concert.
- Remind them to come prepared with hearts primed to pray. On some occasions participants may find it helpful to fast a meal. Leave this to the discretion of each participant.
- Suggest that participants bring friends to the concerts. Encourage them to orient their friends to both the purpose and format of the concerts before they arrive.

You can put your guidelines in writing or just mention some of them at the beginning of a concert event.

One last suggestion: You could distribute a list of issues to be addressed in concerts under fullness and fulfillment, similar to the one that is outlined in the next chapter. You could either give participants an extended list all at once or distribute briefer lists at the end of each concert. With that list you may also include a sample copy of the concert of prayer grid for their own reference.

Such are some of the nuts-and-bolts concerns with which every pacesetter must be concerned. In the next chapter, we want to give tough-minded thinking to expanding our agenda in prayer.

10
AGENDA FOR CONCERTED PRAYER
Shape of Prayers to Come

If, as I have said, the front line in world evangelization is the Word of God and prayer, then the best place to begin growing your prayer agenda is to unearth all that the Scriptures teach on the themes of fullness and fulfillment. You'll find enough issues to keep a concert of prayer breathing and moving forever!

To help you, I suggest that you take two inexpensive Bibles. In one, underline with a pink highlighting pen all the references that have to do with the subject of fullness—you might begin with Isaiah or Ephesians. In the other Bible, underline with a yellow pen all the references that have to do with fulfillment. That might be a good start for your concert of prayer. You can take some of the verses and use them as prayer targets in each concert.

GET IT GROWING

However you do it, it is important that your prayers reflect the biblical dimensions of God's Kingdom. As you study Scripture and then as you meet in concerts of prayer, constantly think about God's intentions for the Church and for the world by asking the following questions to enlarge your prayer concerns:

- What is the scope and content of God's purpose for history, the Church and the nations?
- In specific ways, what would it look like for God's Kingdom, described for us in Scripture, to invade the Church? The world? Your own life?
- How extensive might the impact of His Kingdom grow to be upon His people and His world?
- Why is the fullness of Christ and His Church so essential for the fulfillment of His purposes in the earth?
- How has His purpose unfolded so far?
- Where have there been problems?
- What has been responsible for victories?
- Where are we in God's purposes now? What is left to do? How will it get done?
- Biblically speaking, how can each of us fit in most strategically?

These questions aren't designed to discourage us from praying for personal concerns and issues each of us have. But if we are involved in prayer for spiritual awakening, we must somehow relate even the most personal prayers to the larger scope of God's purposes. How else does one give breadth and depth to prayers that are a part of his or her daily walk? The above questions can help.

Let's keep working at growing our agenda. Try this mind-expanding approach on for size: "If God were to answer your requests—whatever they may be—to the fullest extent you can imagine possible—based on who you know Him to be and what He has said in His Word—what might be the impact of those answers on spiritual awakening—fullness in the Church, fulfillment of the global cause?" Better read that question again!

For instance, let's say you are a college student whose father has recently become unemployed; it appears there may not be enough money for you to stay at school for another quarter. You might have to leave school and go to work. How should you pray about this? Of course, you might pray that God would comfort your father and somehow supply the funds, and that's okay. But using the question I just gave you, you might be led to also pray that God would use this experience in ways that change the world.

How? To teach you and your father new dimensions of trusting Him which later you can share with other Christians to build them up in fullness of faith. Or, you might pray that God will allow you to experience the helplessness and vulnerability that comes with "poverty," as temporary as it may be, long enough to help you to understand something of what life is like for most of the world's unreached peoples and to care for them more deeply.

WHAT ARE THE ISSUES?

The book you hold right now has insights on prayer issues for the Church and the world on almost every single page. I suggest that every committed member of your concert of prayer obtain a copy to refer to when they seek to prime their pump in personal preparation for your next gathering. You might review chapter five, placing a star (*) in the margin at every statement or fact that ought to be addressed in prayer. Then go through the additional issues listed on the next few pages, doing the same. Bring the book with you to upcoming concerts and refer to it during the meeting, picking one or two issues that you will voice in prayer. In addition, you might fuel prayer by reading suggestions from the back of the book.

And don't forget the prayer grid we gave you earlier. Write in awakening issues that currently concern you. How would you fill in each of the 12 triangles if you had to right now? Growing your agenda is simply a matter of the Father helping you add additional items to each triangle as you read, listen, travel and interact with others, and as you press on in prayer yourself.

Scriptures on Fullness and Fulfillment

The following verses are examples of passages that might be briefly discussed at a concert of prayer to get a biblical perspective on prayer issues regarding the Church and the nations.

Exodus 17; 33:7-34:11
Numbers 10:1-10
2 Chronicles 6:12-7:16; 15:1-15
Psalm 102:1-7
Isaiah 59:16-62:7

Jeremiah 33:1-9
Joel 2:12-32
Zechariah 2:10-4:14; 8:20-23
Matthew 9:35-10:1; 18:18-20
Luke 11:1-10
John 14:12-14; 15:5-8; 17
Acts 2:42-47; 4:23-31; 13:1-4
Ephesians 1:15-23; 3:16-21; 6:10-20
1 Timothy 2:1-8
Hebrews 10:19-25,35-11:1; 12:1-2,22-29
1 John 3:18-24; 5:13-15
Revelation 5:8-10; 8:1-5

The rest of this chapter contains a list of issues under fullness and fulfillment which will get you started toward filling out the 12 triangles on your grid. You can add other issues as God teaches you what He wants you and your concert of prayer to cover. At the end of each list is space for you to add areas that you want to pray for which I have missed.

In fact, it is important to always keep asking the Father what He wants you to pray about, no matter how long your own list grows. The direction He wants your next concert of prayer to move might be totally different from your past list of ideas. That is as it should be. After all, He is both composer and conductor.

Issues to Address in Prayer for Fullness

- That God would give a global awakening to His Church, helping us to know Christ well enough so we trust, love and obey Him, so we move with Him in new ways for the fulfillment of His global cause in our generation.
- That the Church would be united in faith, acknowledging Christ as its head in every respect, unveiling His glory before a watching world.
- That the Church would awaken to the universal authority of Christ, which is the basis of her commitment to the advancing of His Kingdom.
- That God would fill us with hope, giving us a clear vision of what the Church is moving toward so that out of that hope would spring faith and love.
- That the Spirit would bring to ultimate fruitfulness and impact

the current renewing work He is already accomplishing in parts of the Body of Christ.

- That the Church would see the need to seek global awakening and renewal for a new mission thrust.
- For God to make us aware of others who have a similar burden for spiritual awakening, so that we might unite our hearts together in prayer.
- For God to raise up many prayer bands of "world Christians" on our campuses, in our churches and mission agencies, and throughout His Church worldwide.
- That God would show us our needs and our weaknesses so thoroughly that we become desperate in our seeking and utterly dependent on Him.
- For God to open us to deeper ministries of the Holy Spirit, so He could be poured out on us as fully as God intends.
- That the Spirit would share with His Church the truths of Christ and reveal Him to us.
- For new awareness of God's holiness and the Church's need to be holy as He is, if we are to have a significant impact for His glory.
- For God to convict us of every area of sin so that we might be led into the holiness of Jesus.
- That God would help those who are praying with us in our concerts of prayer to live a daily life that reflects all we have prayed for together.
- For a fresh sense of God's love for the world, and rekindling of our love for Him.
- That God would give us a new heart of love. That God would move us to seek it until we are willing to take the whole world into our hearts.
- That God would bring reconciliation to His Church, so that all Christians can become transparent before God and each other; that we would unite for the sake of Christ in repentance and forgiveness.
- Wherever there are major rifts and divisions within the Body of Christ, that God would heal those divisions so that the gospel would have greater credibility as the world observes "how we love one another."
- For members of our local church; for our immaturities and

selfish demands that divert our pastor's vision for spiritual awakening and deplete his energies in advancing Christ's Kingdom.

- For the grace to accept every enablement God sends for us for choosing the best, and doing what maximizes Christ's glory.
- That God would forgive us for the times we fail to choose what is just and to do what glorifies Christ.
- That God would convict us of our pride and divisiveness, open our ears and eyes to hear and see one another the way God does, and to help us minister to one another in the power of Christ.
- That God would help us repent of everything that prevents us from following Christ without limits, even to the ends of the earth: sin, unbelief, preoccupation, and self-serving.
- That God would overrule all internal barriers within the Church that would hinder the advancement of the gospel—paralysis of faith, preoccupations, parochialism, and indifference.
- That Christians would be set free to reorganize their lifestyles so that they can better respond to people's deepest needs in effective ways, especially in places where the gospel has not yet come.
- That God would break the hold of money in the life of the Church, and that we would be delivered from its power, allurement, and folly.
- That God would give believers, beginning in our own concert of prayer, transparency with one another, humility, brokenness, and reconciliation wherever it is needed.
- That God would renew our world vision and our faith to move forward to face the challenge of reaching the nations, beginning where we live.
- That God would educate His people about His heart for the world and how He sees the world, so that our acts of obedience would correspond to the facts.
- For the Spirit of God to so empower us as a missionary spirit, that He will make us a missionary Church.
- That God would give IIis people wholehearted zeal for His worldwide purposes.

- That God would deliver us from drifting, aimlessness, and fruitlessness, and set us on a straight and level path in urgency for His Kingdom.
- That the Church worldwide might be unified to fulfill the Great Commission in our generation, especially among the 2.5 billion people who can only be reached by major new effort in cross-cultural evangelism.
- That God would give us such gratitude for all He has done already for us personally and collectively, that we would delight to bring what we have found to those who have never heard.
- For a spirit of "surrender" within the Church and a willingness to do whatever God calls us to do, at whatever price.
- That the Spirit would summon Christians to accountability before Christ in the sharing of our unique blessings in Him with the billions locked away in extreme spiritual and physical poverty. That we would repent of hoarding the gospel, so that we might release its full impact of love and justice worldwide.
- That God would fill His people with hearts of compassion for the earth's unreached, until we come to the place where, like Christ, we are ready to die for them.
- That we would awaken to the world-sized part God has given to each one of us and to His global Church, with our world-sized potential in His plan for the nations.
- That God would help us actively desire to overflow in ministry to the world around and beyond us.
- For God to help us see every "human limitation" or "handicap" as a gift which, once liberated, builds up the Church and advances the Kingdom.
- That God would give mature leadership for the solid discipling of national churches, especially in those countries and among those people where we have recently seen such spiritual vitality and evangelistic ferment—such as Nigeria, Kenya, South Korea, Philippines, India, Brazil, Columbia, Norway, Poland, China, and many others.
- That Christian groups and churches would be awakened with a vision of how God has sovereignly teamed them up, giving them unique experiences and gifts so that together they might fulfill strategic missions that touch the ends of the earth.

- That those being won to Christ around the world right now could immediately sense their calling not only to join themselves to Christ but also to enter wholeheartedly into His global cause.
- That God would raise up pioneers of faith to lead the Church to embrace the new things God wants to do through us in this generation, beginning in prayer.
- That God would raise up godly visionary leaders to take His people on into our mission of redemption and healing among all nations and peoples.
- That God would give many churches and teams around the world new dreams and visions for specific missions to the world.
- That God would help His Church identify the starting place for such dreams: that we would discover the resources and gifts in the Body of Christ and how to use these unique blessings God has given us to share with families of the earth.
- That God would bring commitment to Christ and His global cause among the hundreds of thousands of Christian students worldwide, and prepare them to assume leadership and sacrifice to carry out that commitment.
- That the Church would be filled with victorious optimism in keeping with God's love and purposes for the whole earth, and step forth boldly in the light of that victory, for fulfillment of God's promises through us for this generation.
-
-
-
-

Issues in Praying for Fulfillment

- For God to be glorified throughout the earth, among all people everywhere. Tell Him you want this to happen and tell Him what it will mean to you personally when it does.
- For the climax of history that depends, to a large degree, on the compassionate, Spirit-empowered witness of Christ's worldwide Church.
- That God would receive new praise in the earth, not only for what He is presently doing in the Church, but especially for all

He does through the Church to reach, salvage, and fulfill unreached peoples around the world.

- That Christ's global cause of love and justice will prevail. It is a life or death issue! People without Christ everywhere lack an inheritance in God's Kingdom and have no way to receive His salvation.
- For churches of maturing disciples to be planted within every people group within this generation.
- For bold new thrusts in world evangelization through the intentional, sacrificial penetration of major human barriers worldwide.
- For awakening and spiritual hunger among the 2.5 billion people, such as Muslims, Chinese, Hindus, Buddhists, who have yet to hear of Christ. That they may have a new sense of reality of God and an awakened desire to seek Him.
- For those millions who have heard of Christ and have some understanding of the gospel, including nominal Christians, but have yet to come to full "birth" in a commitment to the Lordship of Christ in their lives. That they may be reborn into faithful and obedient servants of Christ in this generation. If just this one prayer were answered, it would have an unprecedented impact for world evangelization.
- For Satan to be bound and fully routed. That Christ's victory on the cross would break Satan's hold on nations and cultures.
- That God would defeat the diverse strategies of Satan and his kingdom as they manifest themselves through many day-to-day "powers" that often literally enslave multitudes—nationalism, militarism, traditionalism, technocracy, racism, scientism, secularism, expansionism, materialism—and keep them blind to the grace of God.
- For world leaders and governments, and for the outcome of world events. All of these can directly affect the free flowing of the gospel within a nation or within a people-group (1 Tim. 2:1-4).
- That the gospel would have such an impact that the lordship of Christ might be brought to bear on the decisions of earthly rulers. And that in turn, their judgments would bring justice, mercy, and dignity as well as true peace to the nations.
- That God would raise up God-fearing, righteous leaders to be

placed in positions of authority and influence in such areas as government, education, judicial, media, medicine, business, and commerce, as well as in homes and churches.

- For major global issues that impinge upon a world mission thrust and are part of the moral darkness that must be penetrated by the gospel and the planting of responsible communities of disciples among the billions who have yet to hear. Such issues include global hunger, nuclear proliferation, and political and economic oppression.
- For those in prison, the fairness of the judicial system, effective law enforcement, and compassion to victims and families.
- For justice throughout our land, throughout the world, so that people who are made in the image of God would find fair treatment and know the righteousness of God.
- That God would have mercy at every point where we sense that His judgments may be imminent. That His power to curse or bless would become apparent to those who are standing under His judgment.
- That God would overthrow governments that rob their people of basic human rights, oppressing them and exploiting them cruelly, and keeping them from the gospel.
- That God would convict the leaders of the world who hold our planet under the threat of massive destruction; that He would provide wisdom for a way out of this horror.
- For mission agencies, the vessels through which God often thrusts forth laborers into the harvest. Pray that they will be purified and reshaped to channel the new wine of revival to the ends of the earth.
- For God's people everywhere to see those nearby whose ways of living differ from them enough to cut them off from the regular witness of the gospel—to see them and reach them. We need special sensitivity to the poor, oppressed, friendless.
- That individual churches around the world will adopt some of the earth's unreached people groups, taking them as their special focus for prayer and action.
- For specific people groups (there are more than 17,000) beyond the reach of the gospel. Ask God to give your church and His people in many places the wisdom to know how to reach them. Ask God to show: What opportunities now exist?

What barriers stand in the way? What will it take for Christians to cross those barriers? How might Christians best do this now? As He answers, turn those answers into points for further intercession for the specific group and your group's role in serving them.

- That God would give to the Church the gift of "apostles" (1 Cor. 12:28). We need hundreds of thousands of cross-cultural messengers to be sent out by churches around the world. Ask God to give the Church wisdom to know who these people are, to set them apart for the work to which He has called them, and to send them forth by a movement of prayer and sacrifice.

- That God would deploy a new force of self-supporting (tent-making) witnesses to relocate among those people of the earth closed to professional missionary outreach. That lay people would get a vision for this for themselves.

- For all current efforts to research and formulate mission strategy, to effectively deploy a new generation of missionaries.

- For technical areas of mission outreach such as Bible translation, Bible correspondence courses, Christian radio and TV, theological education by extension (TEE), saturation evangelism, student work worldwide, medical mission relief and aid ministries, and short-term missions.

- Since a major aspect of Jesus' ministry to the unreached involved the casting out of demons, the healing of the lame and the deaf and the blind, the raising of the dead, and many other miracles, ask God to give His Church worldwide whatever signs and wonders are needed to confirm the Word before an unbelieving world.

- Pray for those who are either accessible to a Christian witness from the outside, or who are responsive to whatever witness is already there but which needs more workers.

- That God would help us be keenly aware of the opportunities He is giving us now to testify of Christ to the unreached world.

- For those people and places where the doors are open for hundreds of additional laborers to enter. That the doors would remain open and that workers would soon be found to walk through them.

- For the Christian Church within every country. That God would raise up out of revival a new mission thrust from every nation and people-group where communities of disciples already exist.
- That God would raise up men and women with specific gifts and proven experience in training and evangelism who will be able to work in conjunction with local churches in host countries, or with other missionaries.
- For suffering Christians who often experience temptations, oppressions, and persecutions because they aggressively operate with the gospel in the whirlpool created by two diametrically opposed spiritual powers. Pray especially for those facing increased dangers from revolutions and terrorism.
- For specific missionary movements in the third world. Today, there are 15,000 Third World missionaries sent out by more than 300 Third World agencies.
- For specific evangelical North American missionary societies. For their organizational and personnel needs, and for particular outreaches and mission projects.
- For America as a major sending base of missionary personnel. Of the 80,000 Protestant missionaries worldwide, almost 60,000 come from North America. Pray that God would revive the Church in our nation so that the base of Christians here, containing 80 percent of the evangelical resources of the world and 70 percent of its trained Christians, might continue to release these God-given blessings for ministry to the earth's unreached. Pray that the revival will enrich the quality of the missionaries who go.
- For the unreached "nations" in America. The unique United States ethno-cultural panorama includes 120 ethnic groups speaking over 100 different languages. At least 3 million in the United States have no knowledge of Christ and no one near them who is like them to tell them of Christ. Tens of millions more, many locked away among the urban poor of our cities, are out of touch with compassionate, witnessing Christians, or see little credibility in the gospel.
- For the 300,000 international students on our campuses, many from the major "closed" countries. For the millions of international visitors in the United States every year.

- For God to raise up a new movement of "senders" worldwide—people who know God has called them to send a new force of cross-cultural witnesses and who embrace that assignment with the same vision and sacrifices as those who go.
-
-
-
-

So you see, growing your prayer agenda for a concert isn't all that hard. In fact, it is quite exciting! Combining all the issues gleaned from Scripture, expanding your current prayer list so that personal requests reflect dimensions of fullness and fulfillment, and gradually adding newer issues to your prayer strategy, as the above empty spaces suggest, will remain right on target for revival. You'll certainly not get bored!

To take a practical first step right now, return to the "grid" in chapter 8 and, using the 12 triangles it gives you, fill in each with one prayer issue from the suggestions in this chapter.

11
HEY, LEADER
STRIKE UP THE BAND
Marching Out in a Concert of Prayer

If fellowship with the Father and Son is like walking in the light (1 John 1:5-7), then a concert of prayer is like a group of Christians, in fellowship with God and each other, who have formed a marching band in the light—a parade set loose in the courts of heaven, marching to the ends of the earth. Is this similar to what Paul had in mind when he wrote of armies of pray-ers in Ephesians 6?

What are the paces our Leader wants to put us through? What beat do we march to? In this final chapter, you'll get answers that will take your concerts of prayer off toward the sunrise of spiritual awakening like one grand victory procession.

THE THREE PACES OF INTERCESSION

Recently I strolled in the gardens of Pembroke College, one of 35 colleges that make up Oxford University in England. As a young man, George Whitefield studied at Pembroke. There he was converted and joined in the fellowship of concerted prayer called the "holy club," that included the Wesleys.

Near the oldest building of the college stand three statues, depicting key aspects of prayer. The first figure is seated with its head in its hands, thinking of things eternal. The second is on his knees, hands clasped, arms outstretched toward heaven.

The third figure stands erect, with shield and sword, ready to do battle. As I looked at these three figures, I recalled the force of prayer in the ministry of George Whitefield himself and thought of the three paces of intercession the Lord brings us through when He calls us to strike up a concert of prayer. They are solidarity, advocacy, and pursuit.

Like the seated statue, part of intercession is coming into agreement with God, pondering on what He wants and then desiring it with Him—in other words, solidarity. At other times intercession, like the kneeling figure, calls us to bleed with the Father, particularly on behalf of those situations and peoples where others will not or cannot pray. So, we become advocates for them. But then on some issues God calls us to march into a real battle, to press His purposes forward with unflagging zeal and at any cost until we see accomplished what He has burdened us to pray for. Pursuing prayer takes over at this point.

These intensifying paces are endorsed in our Lord's teaching. Sometimes He told us to ask—simply agreeing with God; sometimes to seek, which includes doing so on behalf of others; and sometimes to knock, clearly the most aggressive of the three and the most demanding.

SOLIDARITY: AGREEING WITH GOD
In solidarity, we align ourselves, in prayer, with what God has shown us in His Word and agree with Him saying, "Father, we want what you want." As Martin Luther defined it: "Prayer is not overcoming God's reluctance; it is laying hold of his highest willingness." A friend of mine calls it "jumping on God's bandwagon." Praying in solidarity recognizes that the only thing beyond the reach of our prayers is anything outside the will of God.

Here is where praying "in Jesus' name" finds its true meaning. This is not a phrase to be tacked on at the end to indicate that our prayer is finished. Jesus meant for us to pray with the authority that comes from linking our standing before the Father with Christ's standing, our character with His character, and our reputation with His. We are saying "Father, your Son's life-perspectives, His life-directions, and His life-mission are ours; they shape everything we're asking you to do." For in the final analysis, prayer is a Person—we are allied with the risen Christ. When we ask in His name, we can never want too much from the Father (John 14:16).

In solidarity praying, then, we identify first of all not with the world's battery of needs and longings, but with Jesus' desire to please the Father. God's kingdom must control our agenda in prayer, not what culture defines for us as possible or impossible, but what God said will actually *be*.

Solidarity praying calls us to pray with a desire that every dimension of the new heaven and the new earth may be brought to pass. As we pray for specific Kingdom concerns for our world—such as justice, peace, reconciliation, and wholeness— we should do so with words that anticipate a full breakthrough of God's Kingdom. We should want all of what God wants, and be willing to say so—now!

If you study the great prayers of the Scripture, you will see that, in almost every case, the individual was aligning himself or herself and the people and situations, with the will of God. It is as if each one surveyed past ways and promises of God, took a sounding on what God was doing in the present, gained perspective on where He was headed in the future, and then asked, "How can we be joined with our Father in the past, present, and future of His will? And how can we show this by the way we pray?"

In the same way, we too must be careful not to push our own agenda on God. We must spend time, first of all, listening, waiting, learning from Him, conforming our agenda to His, and then with boldness and joy, coming to agreement.

This was the pattern in Acts 4 when the early Church stood up to persecution by united prayer. Luke tells us they were able to pray with one voice. How did a Church that size pray with such unity? A study of the prayer itself (4:24-30) shows that they took time to discuss both the Word and the situation before they spoke to God.

Here is a key point at which praise and thanksgiving assume prominence. In solidarity praying, praise becomes a critical expression of where we stand vis-à-vis the will of God. You will recall that one of the three approaches to fullness and fulfillment praying on the grid is "rejoice"—both praise and thanksgiving.

True intercession is itself an act of worship and praise. We are telling our Father how much His glory, desires, and purposes mean to us. We are saying that we are so committed to His Son that we want all He has to give of Himself to His church and to His world. Saint Anthony said: "We pray as much as we desire, we desire as much as we love." In solidarity praying we are cleaving to the Father in love (Ps. 91:14).

Learning to pray in solidarity with the Father was Jesus' desire for us. When the disciples came to Him, asking Him to teach them how to pray, they weren't asking for an all-day seminar on prayer. "Teach us how to pray" meant: "Jesus, Master, we have watched you praying for the past two years, and we see how fully in line your prayers are with your Father. Teach us how to pray in a way that is fully in line with who you are and how you pray." Jesus gave them a solidarity prayer, often called the "Lord's Prayer." Not one that said, "Thy will be changed," but rather, "Thy will be done." "God is bound to answer every prayer that conforms to this pattern. Can our prayers be brought within the scope of this prayer? Then it is certain of answer, for the pattern is divinely given."[1]

The Lord's Prayer breaks down into two major parts. The first three requests deal with fulfillment concerns; the second three deal with fullness. Each of the leading verbs in the Greek are in the imperative, almost as if Jesus is giving us permission to command God. How can He do that? Because He knows that to pray along these lines is to be in total harmony with what God is already prepared to do.

ADVOCACY: STANDING UP FOR OTHERS

During and after the Vietnam War, many Americans wore bracelets called "MIA (Missing in Action) bracelets." Each person wore his or her bracelet until the missing serviceman was found. We were advocates for those in enemy hands who could not advocate for themselves.

That is a good model for the second pace of intercessory prayer: advocacy. Having first aligned ourselves with God and His Word, we next align ourselves with those who cannot pray for themselves.

Andrew Murray said, "My drawing nigh to God is of one

piece with my intercourse with men and earth." Out of intimacy with Christ comes responsibility for others, in prayer. Out of love for God, advocacy becomes an act of love for our neighbors. Like the second statue at Pembroke College, advocacy is love pleading on its knees. We begin to see that God intends prayer to be a way for us to release His loving power into the lives of others.

If we are going to take the power of advocacy seriously then we need to deepen our understanding of those for whom we pray and for others who need our prayers. We need to develop intelligently targeted compassion. This is what Jesus had in mind in Matthew 9 when, out of His own compassion, He called His disciples to look clearly at the people in need, then to pray on behalf of those who could not or would not pray for themselves.

A model of intelligently targeted compassion is given to us by Daniel's prayer in Daniel 9. In it he goes over his situation with the Lord, almost like arguing his case in a divine courtroom on behalf of his people Israel, and on behalf of the nations who mock their disgrace. For us too, there may be no higher honor we bestow on God than to clearly and logically unfold our case for His Kingdom as it touches critical needs of the Church and the nations today. I have found *Operation World* and the *World Christian Encyclopedia* very helpful tools as I follow Daniel's model in my advocating. They almost function like a lawyer's brief for me.

Advocating prayers bear directly on the two-fold agenda for concerts. Take the fullness dimension of spiritual awakening for example. Scripture encourages us, not only to identify God's people and their needs, but to advocate changes as God works in His Church. As we pray for fullness we need to be praying "for all of us," even if we are praying repentance prayers that may not seem to directly apply to actions we have taken. When God gives us insights into the needs of other Christians, He does not give them so that we might criticize them but so we might advocate on their behalf and ours.

We also need to advocate regarding the fulfillment of God's purposes among unbelievers. Have you ever supported someone who was helpless, who was depending on you to guide them, feed them, or run their errands? In the same way, we come to the aid of those who are spiritually helpless. Our prayers stand in the gap between unbelievers and the God who loves them as we intercede that they might see and understand clearly who Jesus is. Proverbs 31:8-9 says, "Speak up for those who cannot speak for themselves, for the rights of all who are destitute. Speak up and judge fairly; defend the rights of the poor and the needy." Prayer for those under God's judgment who cannot speak up for themselves is their greatest hope.

PURSUIT: PRESSING ON FOR A CHANGE

Not long ago David Wells stunned some of us with an article in *Christianity Today* titled, "Prayer: Rebellion Against the Status Quo." Did you ever think of prayer that way? As Jesus observed, the Kingdom of God forcefully advances as forceful men lay hold of it (see Matt. 11:12). Does this ever happen through prayer? If so, could we call such prayer rebellion? The answer is yes.

Out of the paces of solidarity and advocacy may come, on some issues, a more intense tempo that feels and looks like one of rebellion. In these cases, God has assigned us the specific responsibility of pursuing Him relentlessly until His will is carried out in full. In so doing, we are saying to Him, "Father the time has come for you to act. There must be delay no longer. You have convinced us that you are ready. Accordingly, we will press on in prayer until you bring the change."

Maybe this is what some mean when they talk about having a burden in prayer. There are some issues under fullness and fulfillment that may burden an individual, or even a whole concert of prayer, and we are not able to shake them. Then it must be borne. Maybe this is what others mean by "the prayer of faith": God gives us the faith to believe that He is ready to move, so much so that we cannot stop asking Him to do it until it happens.

In any case, pursuing prayer is prayer on a mission. It is diligent, fervent, constant, persevering, determined, and convinced! This praying comes closest to the Greek words used for prayer in the New Testament that translate "to petition," "to beg," "to express with a cry." As Luther said of his house dog: "If only I could pray the way my dog looks at the morsel on my plate, all his thoughts concentrated on it."

Prayer that pursues is, by other terms, prayer that "longs." In Romans 8, we are told that in the same way that creation groans to be set free, God's children groan for their resurrection bodies. Even so, the Spirit when He prays for God's purposes in creation and the Church to be fulfilled, does so with groanings that cannot be uttered. Sometimes, the same Holy Spirit leads us to pray for things we are convinced, for God's glory, we ourselves cannot live without. Our longing may be for His work among others in the Body of Christ or for a particular ministry to the world.

Prayer as Suffering

Pursuing prayer becomes a ministry of suffering. I begin to learn how to hurt and cry about the things that break God's heart. This may be the most significant experience any of us will have of fellowship in Christ's travails. The anguish we feel may go beyond words. Here is where fasting as well begins to make real sense. We may literally lose our appetites, or may want to use mealtime to pray.

It is necessary for all of us to ponder what it could cost us to get serious with the Father in concerted prayer. What we pray for we must also be ready to die for. In some ways, the praying may be the first phase in the laying down of our lives in some specific way for Christ's sake and the gospel's.

Prayer as Renewal

There will be pursuant prayer toward the fullness dimension of spiritual awakening. On some issues we will cry out to God day and night, that He might deliver His elect (Luke 18:6-8). We will pray for God to lead a broken and helpless Church out of defeat and into victory for His Son.

Prayer as Intercession

We will also pursue God on behalf of the nations. In pursuant prayer we reach the sharpest edge of front lines work in world evangelization. A friend of mine who took a tour of missionary work stations throughout the Muslim world returned with a startling revelation: wherever he found the gospel making inroads in Muslim communities, he found missionaries who were giving themselves to hours of intercessory prayer each day—pursuant prayer.

What might happen in your concert of prayer as God moves you toward pursuant prayer for the nations? He might lead you to "adopt" particular people groups that have yet to be reached for the gospel. This, in fact, was part of the strategy in prayer mobilization explored recently at the International Prayer Assembly in Korea. As your prayer concert learns solidarity and advocacy, you might find yourselves led by God's Spirit to believe, for example, that He was ready now to penetrate a Muslim refugee enclave in London with the gospel of Christ. What if your concert began to pursue the advancement of Christ's Kingdom in this situation with the same intensity it would pursue missionary work among the refugees if you were suddenly sent out as a team to work with them? Such has actually happened. What if God raised up hundreds of movements of prayer within our nation alone to focus in that way on specific unreached peoples? The potential is thrilling.

Like a band on parade, your concert of prayer marches forth in an aggressive ministry of intercession. The Leader, who has struck up the band, may put you through different paces and different tempos at different times:

- Solidarity: Agreeing with God. "Father, we want what you want."
- Advocacy: Standing up for others. "Father, they need what you have."
- Pursuit: Pressing on for a change. "Father, the time has come for you to act."

Your responsibility and mine is to be sure that we keep in step, side by side, as our instruments blend together in one great fanfare of victory.

Eventually, like a triumphal procession, the concert will bring forth the sweet fragrance of Christ in spiritual awakening (2 Cor. 2). And it will become apparent that ultimately you paraded for the sake of the world—you marched to the ends of the earth.

Did I just hear someone blow a whistle?

Postscript

TRY THE NEXT SEVEN YEARS, FOR A START!

Jonathan Edwards, a New England Puritan visionary and author of *An Humble Attempt,* once presented his generation with a challenge: Meet in monthly concerts of prayer on a sustained basis for seven years, he instructed. Then, pause to evaluate what God has done, to determine if you should keep on.

Seven years? In our "instant" society that may seem preposterous. After all, it is hard enough to convince most of us to be consistent on anything for seven weeks!

But Edwards was onto something that every concert of prayer must face. The Father may not choose to make spiritual awakening visible the very first time we pray for it. And for some time, despite our prayers, many peoples of earth may remain cloistered in darkness.

We are not to be shaken by this, however. God has called us to be faithful in prayer, first of all. Christ's Kingdom will come. But we must rally to Him fully enough (Col. 1:18-20) that even though His global cause seems to advance painfully slow, we still do nothing less, in love for Him and each other, than to keep on praying—for fullness and fulfillment. That is what love demands. Edwards understood.

And yet we remain faithful in hope. Ultimately—even if it be after seven years—our united appeal to the Father will intensify and accelerate the Kingdom's coming. The morning will dawn for our generation. With healing power, Christ will reveal Himself grandly in the midst of His Church before the eyes of the nations as the hope of glory (Col. 1:27). To that end we must struggle in prayer with all the energy God gives us (Col. 1:28–2:3; 4:12).

Anyone out there besides Edwards want to join me in a concert of prayer? . . . for the next (gulp) seven years?

Where can you begin? Meeting 15 minutes a week with your closest friends is a good step. For those of us who are married, the starting place can be—should be—our spouses and families. If unity with our spouses is a guarantee that our prayers are effective (1 Pet. 3:7), then surely sharing a concert of prayer with them—even if only five minutes a day—is a proper path towards such unity.

The point is that we *must* begin. And the time has come. Gathering at the threshold remains our highest priority (1 Tim. 2:1-8).

PACESETTERS
Small Group Study Guide

Welcome, potential pacesetter! The term "pacesetter" comes from chapter 6. You may want to read it now to find out who you might become by the end of these studies of *Concerts of Prayer.*

The seven sessions are designed for those who think God might want them to help mobilize concerted prayer and need to talk it through with others. Ideally your group should consist of 5-8 potential pacesetters. The more you have the less time each has to participate in the discussions.

Each session lasts 90 minutes in order to achieve maximum discussion. The time suggestions below reflect the practicality of this approach. Of course, the sessions can be explored in a variety of settings, such as during a weekly meeting, over seven Saturday morning gatherings, or in total throughout a single weekend retreat.

The discussion facilitator should be familiar with the book and this Study Guide before Session I begins. All group members, however, should have read the "Introduction" to the book before the first meeting.

Each 90-minute session contains the following segments:

    I. *Prayer Passage* (15 min.). Read the assigned verses

and then discuss these 5 questions each time:

   a. What prompted the prayer movement described here?

   b. What can you learn about important characteristics of a prayer movement? Be specific.

   c. What focus and impact did this prayer movement have on God's people?

   d. What focus and impact did this prayer movement have on the nations?

   e. What are two or three principles that you could apply from this passage to a united prayer movement today? Discuss either in terms of one in which you're involved, or one which you would like to encourage into being.

II. *Prayer Time* (15 min.). In each session, begin your opening prayer time by quietly reviewing the list of possible prayer targets at the end of chapter 10. Each group member should select one issue for himself/herself under "Fullness" and under "Fulfillment." Then, spend the remainder of the 15 minutes praying over your selections. Pray as well in response to the passage and for the session itself.

III. *Study* (50 min.). Questions are listed below for each session, with time suggestions for each period of discussion.

IV. *Mini-Concert of Prayer* (10 min.). By using insights, challenges and visions generated in your study, fuel your united prayer for spiritual awakening and world evangelization.

V. *Assignment.* Be sure to be faithful to the Lord and your group by thoughtfully reading the assigned chapters for the next session. If you do these sessions on a single weekend retreat, however, the whole book should be completed beforehand.

SESSION I

Prayer Passage: Acts 1:1-14; 2:1-21 (15 min.)
Prayer Time: Fullness and Fulfillment (50 min.)
Study of Introduction (to be read beforehand) (50 min.)

1. What is your most positive experience with corporate prayer? Why was it so positive? (5 min.)
2. What is your most discouraging experience with corporate prayer? What could have made it more meaningful? (5 min.)
3. What do you hope to gain from these sessions for your personal prayer life? (3 min.)
4. In what ways do you hope to use your discoveries from these sessions to actively assist efforts at united prayer? (3 min.)
5. This book is about "concerts of prayer." The term stimulates musical imagery. Draw as many parallels from the world of music to united prayer as you can. For example: Jesus "conducts" us as we pray together. (3 min.)
6. How do these parallels suggest the possibility of new and exciting dimensions to prayer for you? (3 min.)
7. Take an overview of the "Contents" at the front of the book. Which chapter seems to fascinate you the most right now? Why? Which one looks most promising for you? (5 min.)
8. Read the covenant suggested on page 167. Can you imagine yourself being part of a prayer movement that captures the spirit of this covenant? If so, how might it differ from other prayer experiences you have had in the past? (9 min.)
9. Let's experiment with your current prayer life. What are the two most significant prayer requests you've focused on personally over the past month? Share one of them with the group. Then, determine how you would respond to this question: If God were to answer this one area to the fullest extent I could imagine possible—based on what He has said in His word and who I know Him to be—what might be the impact of that answer for Christ's global cause? (This helps to illustrate something of the unique focus of a concert of prayer.) Discuss your responses. Then ask: What if you

started to pray this way about everything, every day? What if you were united with others who prayed the same way? What differences might this make? (14 min.)

Mini-Concert of Prayer (10 min.)
Assignment for Session II: Read chapters 1 and 2.

SESSION II

Prayer Passage: Psalm 102:1-22 (15 min.)
Prayer Time: Fullness and Fulfillment (15 min.)
Study of Chapter 1 and 2 (50 min.)

1. In what ways do you sometimes feel like an "ordinary person"? How does David's opening parable give you new perspective on yourself? Do you have any hope that God might be willing to surprise you this way? Describe it (5 min.)
2. What evidences do you see around you of tremors that suggest we may be on the verge of a new shaking in the Church—of spiritual awakening? Be specific. (3 min.)
3. Read Richard Lovelace's statement on page 33. Do you agree? Why or why not? (3 min.)
4. Discuss your reactions to the five "theses" outlined on page 41. Where do you agree or disagree? If all of us could agree, what practical differences would that make for us or for the Church at large? (10 min.)
5. Suggest some differences and unique benefits which can be found in concerted (corporate) prayer over private prayer. Then discuss: Do you sense that today concerted prayer needs to be restored to its priority in the Church? Why or why not? (8 min.)
6. What do you understand to be the distinctives of a concert of prayer over other kinds of prayer experiences? Why would it be important to keep these distinctives in clear view? (10 min.)
7. In light of what God is doing to mobilize concerted prayer worldwide, what would be an important next step for you to take? For your study group to take? (11 min.)

Mini-Concert of Prayer (10 min.)
Assignment for Session III: Read chapters 3 and 4.

SESSION III

Prayer Passage: Hosea 5:13–6:3; 14:1-9 (15 min.)
Prayer Time: Fullness and Fulfillment (15 min.)
Study of Chapters 3 and 4 (50 min.)

1. Name a time in your own life when you felt yourself to be in the same discouraging position as the remnant group to whom God sent Zechariah. How did you handle it? How was your approach like or unlike the one envisioned in Zechariah 8? (5 min.)
2. Consider the four hallmarks of a united prayer movement— attitude, agenda, impact, ignition. Discuss: Do these seem comprehensive enough to you? Why or why not? Describe how you might expect them to unfold in your own situation (such as your church, campus fellowship, city or organization). Be specific. Then answer: Would God be willing to make this vision a reality in your situation? Why or why not? (10 min.)
3. How would you define "spiritual awakening"? Write out a two-three sentence definition using your own words. Then, share your definitions with one another. Discuss: How are your definitions similar? How do they differ? How do the differences help to round out each individual definition? (10 min.)
4. Now read the definitions provided in chapter 4 by J. Edwin Orr, Richard Lovelace and David Bryant. Discuss: How are they similar? How do they differ? How do the differences help to round out each individual definition? Finally: What do these three definitions add to the ideas your group compiled under question 3 above? What do your ideas add to *them*? (15 min.)
5. In light of all your discussions in this session, how convinced are *you* of the need for spiritual awakening in the Church today? If, in answer to a united prayer movement in which you participated, God were to grant spiritual awakening—

what changes might that bring to your life? What changes might it bring to your Christian group or fellowship?

Mini-Concert of Prayer (10 min.)
Assignment for Session IV: Read chapter 5.

SESSION IV

Prayer Passage: 2 Chronicles 15 (15 min.)
Prayer Time: Fullness and Fulfillment (15 min.)
Study of Chapter 5 (50 min.)

1. Define the word "hope." Describe the last time you had a personal experience of hope. (5 min.)
2. David outlines four good reasons why we should hope for and pray toward spiritual awakening: the divine pattern, the dark prospects, the disturbing paralysis and the dramatic preparations. Take each one separately. Spend 10 minutes discussing each one using the following questions:
   a. How would you summarize this reason in two or three sentences? Does it give us hope?
   b. What about it is still not clear to you? Where do you have questions on it?
   c. What additional evidences of it do you see, beyond what David describes?
   d. How might all of this change the way we pray individually and corporately?

3. What evidences do you see of these four reasons—pattern, prospects, paralysis, preparations *right around you?* What reasons do *you* have to hope for and pray toward spiritual awakening? (5 min.)

Mini-Concert of Prayer (10 min.)
Assignment for Session V: Read chapters 6 and 7.

SESSION V

Prayer Passage: Joel 1:5-14; 2:11-25 (15 min.)
Prayer Time: Fullness and Fulfillment (15 min.)
Study of Chapters 6 and 7 (50 min.)

1. Working together, draw up a list of as many synonyms (either words or phrases) as you can of the word "pacesetter." Then discuss: Is this a role you want to assume in an emerging God-given movement of united prayer? (5 min.)
2. Next discuss how ready you feel you are to assume a pacesetter's "statement of intent" similar in spirit to the one below:
    "By the grace of God, for Christ's glory and in the Spirit's strength, it is my wholehearted intention to encourage and assist concerted prayer for spiritual awakening and world evangelization in the Christian fellowship to which God sends me."
    Discuss: What appears possible for *you* in such a statement? What looks too overwhelming or challenging for you right now? How would you rewrite it to better express the role you believe God has given you at the moment? (10 min.)
3. How would you define the word "repentance"? What are areas where you need to repent as a step toward concerted prayer? What are areas where your Christian fellowship may need to do so? Be specific. (8 min.)
4. Do you believe the kind of unity in prayer about which David writes is really possible in your situation (fellowship, church, city, organization)? Why or why not? What is possible right now? Be specific. (8 min.)
5. How are you currently preparing yourself to be as fully involved in spiritual awakening and world evangelization as God will allow you? Does this preparation involve a daily discipline that reflects what you are praying for? Describe this for the group. What do you think of David's suggestions for a daily discipline? (8 min.)
6. In what ways do you see the steps of repentance, unity and

discipline to be important in anyone's attempts to help mobilize concerted prayer? What can you do to encourage such steps in your efforts at mobilizing prayer? (11 min.)

Mini-Concert of Prayer (10 min.)
Assignment for Session VI: Read chapters 8 and 9.

SESSION VI

Prayer Passage: Acts 4:1-4, 23-31 (15 min.)
Prayer Time: Fullness and Fulfillment (15 min.)
Study of Chapters 8 and 9 (50 min.)

1. In the past, what things have most discouraged you away from aggressive, consistent, personal prayer? Be specific. Do you know others who have experienced the same things? Describe why facing these issues yourself can help you mobilize others into concerted prayer. (8 min.)
2. David presents 15 principles for mobilizing concerted prayer. Discuss any eight of them very briefly, using these three questions: Does this principle look like it would work in your situation? Why or why not? If it does, what would be one important next step you could take to implement it? (15 min.)
3. Do you see any possibilities of forming a steering committee to help guide a united prayer movement in your area? If so, discuss briefly how it might happen. (5 min.)
4. Do you see any possibilities of sponsoring a consultation on concerted prayer in your area? If so, discuss briefly how it might happen. (5 min.)
5. Have you ever led a united prayer meeting before? If so, which ideas discussed in chapter 9 did you follow? Which ideas do you *wish* you had known? Discuss one or two ideas apiece, and do so briefly. (10 min.)
6. What do you think of the Concert of Prayer format suggested on page 173: How would you like to alter it to more effectively fit your situation or your group? (5 min.)
7. As this session closes, do you feel better equipped to become a pacesetter? (2 min.)

Mini-Concert of Prayer (10 min.)
Assignment for Session VII: Read chapters 10 and 11 and "Postscript."

SESSION VII

Prayer Passage: Luke 11:1-13 (15 min.)
Prayer Time: Fullness and Fulfillment (15 min.)
Study of Chapters 10 and 11 and "Postscript" (50 min.)

1. What are additional issues your study group could add to the preliminary listing David provides in chapter 10 under the heading "Fullness"? And also, under "Fulfillment"? As a group, try to come up with 3-4 additional issues under each heading. (8 min.)
2. How have you personally experienced the three paces in intercession outlined by David in chapter 11? Be specific. Have you experienced them more in praying for fullness issues or fulfillment issues? Why is this? In what ways do you sense any need for growth in this area? (10 min.)
3. What difference could it make during a time of concerted prayer if each of us were able to recognize these three paces and how they work together? How might our ministry of corporate intercession become more effective? (5 min.)
4. As we end these seven study sessions, what do you sense to be the most strategic next step you could take individually? What might be steps two and three? (10 min.)
5. Do you sense that God has any assignment for your study group to carry out together in response to all you've explored in these sessions? If so, what? If so, when? If so, how? If so, why? (17 min.)

Mini-Concert of Prayer (10 min.)
Post-Study Assignment: Look over the Appendices and Bibliography. Then do the next thing God shows you to do!

AGENDA
FOR
CONSULTATION ON
CONCERTS OF PRAYER

(Place)

(Date)

(Time)

This is what the Lord Almighty says: "Many peoples and the inhabitants of many cities will yet come, and the inhabitants of one city will go to another and say, 'Let us go at once to entreat the Lord and seek the Lord Almighty. I myself am going.' In those days ten from all languages and nations will take firm hold of one Jew by the edge of his robe and say, 'Let us go with you, because we have heard that God is with you.'"
—Zechariah 8:20-23

Introduction
Welcome ....5 minutes
Scripture Reading.........................5 minutes
United Hymn and Prayer Time ....15 minutes

Overview of the Consultation: Purpose and Agenda..5 minutes

Introductions of Consultation Participants . . . . 15 minutes
Case Studies of Current Prayer Movements . . . . 45 minutes

Discussion of the Three Proposals

Presentation of *Proposal #1*—"A Call for Concerts of Prayer" . . . . 10 min.
Discussion of Proposal #1—What are the needs and opportunities for Concerts of Prayer? . . . . 35 min.

Presentation of *Proposal #2*—"A Strategy for Mobilizing Concerts of Prayer" . . . . 10 min.

Discussion of Proposal #2—What is the best approach for mobilizing Concerts of Prayer? . . . . 50 min.

Break for Lunch . . . . 50 min.

Presentation of *Proposal #3*—"A Cooperative Plan of Action for Concerts of Prayer" . . . . 15 min.
Discussion of Proposal #3—How can we cooperate in practical terms to co-sponsor and assist local Concerts of Prayer? . . . . 75 min.

Break . . . . 15 min.

Forming a Cooperative Plan of Action

Summary of discussions on Proposals 1,2,3 . . . . 10 min.
Discussion: Where do we have consensus for a plan of action? . . . . 60 min.

* On a time frame for coordinating Concerts?
* On an approach toward co-sponsorship of local Concerts?
* On an approach toward cooperative assistance of local Concerts?
* On ways to measure the quality and impact of local Concerts?

* On a *facilitating* body (such as a steering committee)?
* On immediate steps following this Consultation?

Statement of Action: Confirmation of a joint committee to a
   cooperative plan of action.....................30 min.

Conclusion

Mini-Concert of Prayer ....30 min.
Depart to fulfill our commitments

WORKING PROPOSALS FOR CONSULTATION

Based on our common vision for and commitment to united prayer for spiritual awakening and world evangelization, the following three proposals are set forth:

PROPOSAL ONE—A Call for Concerts of Prayer

In view of the great needs facing the Church internally, for revival and awakening;

And, in view of the great needs facing the Church externally, for the evangelization of the world and the worldwide advancement of Christ's Kingdom;

And, in view of the unprecedented opportunities calling the Church to seek Christ's fullness in our life together, for the fulfillment of His global mission;

And, recognizing that the prelude to and sustaining foundation for a new work of God in the Church is united prayer for spiritual awakening and world evangelization;

And, borrowing from history a term used to describe similar movements of united prayer during previous spiritual awakenings (Concerts of Prayer);

it is proposed that we here this day commit ourselves as Christian leaders to one another and the Church, to call for and to help mobilize local concerts of prayer for spiritual awakening and world evangelization.

PROPOSAL TWO—A Strategy for Mobilizing Concerts of Prayer

Based on our commitment to call for and assist Concerts of Prayer within the Church in our nation;

And, drawing from the praying constituents of national organizations and ministries within the three major spheres of churches, students and mission;

And, looking to local prayer leadership and prayer movements to

help steer and galvanize these praying people into grass-
roots efforts at Concerts of Prayer;
it is proposed that we here this day, as Christian leaders, cooperate in encouraging and serving our praying people by endorsing
and co-sponsoring local concerts of prayer. Linking with local
prayer leaders, we will assist our praying people into concerts of
prayer within our own community.

PROPOSAL THREE—A Cooperative Plan of Action for Concerts of Prayer

Rising from consensus on the call for Concerts of Prayer (Proposal 1) and the strategy for mobilizing Concerts of Prayer (Proposal 2), *it is proposed* that we here as Christian leaders take
immediate steps toward co-sponsorship of local Concerts of
Prayer over the next two years. To be more precise, *it is proposed:*
1. That between (date) and (date), (total number) jointly-
sponsored concerts of prayer for spiritual awakening and world
evangelization be initiated and assisted where local prayer leadership is already evident.
2. That the movement of prayer be developed in at least four
phases:
* Concert of Prayer *endorsement:* local leaders and organiza-
    tions in the major spheres of churches, students and mis-
    sions make direct contact with their praying constituents,
    explaining the concert of prayer strategy and encouraging
    them to become part of a concert of prayer in their com-
    munity.
* Concert of Prayer *event:* Leaders and organizations in the
    major spheres of churches, students and mission coordi-
    nate with local prayer leaders and prayer committees to
    draw together their praying constituents into one initial
    concert of prayer within their own community.
* Concert of Prayer *movement:* As a result of the endorsements
    and rising from the event, on-going, community-wide con-
    certs of prayer emerge under the leadership of a local,
    trans-denominational steering committee, in cooperation
    with the mobilizing efforts of leaders and organizations
    from the three major spheres.

* Concert of Prayer *nurture*: In counsel with leaders and endorsing organizations in the three major spheres, the local steering committee work to sharpen, encourage, strengthen and expand the community-wide concert of prayer.

3. That, where appropriate, every effort be made to expand the base of supportive, co-sponsoring individuals and organizations.

4. That commitment and accountability for the concerts be kept primarily under the guidance of the local steering committee.

5. That evaluation of the concert of prayer movement be made by sponsoring groups, determining the impact on their own internal objectives with respect to spiritual awakening and world outreach. This should be done at specific checkpoints culminating in a major evaluation by (date), possibly through another community-wide consultation.

6. That helpful contact should be made with the National Prayer Committee (address below) which may suggest resources, facilitate some training, and provide information on the prayer movement nationwide.

For further help on such a consultation, write to:

> National Prayer Committee
> Concert of Prayer Project
> 233 Langdon Street
> Madison, WI 53703

A sample copy of a camera-ready "Invitation to a Concert of Prayer" is also available from the above address.

A CALL TO PRAYER FOR SPIRITUAL AWAKENING AND WORLD EVANGELIZATION FROM THE 1984 INTERNATIONAL PRAYER ASSEMBLY, SEOUL, KOREA

God, in His Providence, has brought us together in Seoul, Korea, from 69 nations. We have sought His face and His guidance. He has impressed on us an urgent desire to call for an international prayer movement for spiritual awakening and world evangelization.

Theological Basis

World evangelization is a sovereign work of the triune God through the ministry of Christ's church. The forces of darkness which block the spread of truth and the growth of the church cannot be displaced by human plans and efforts. Only the omnipotent Holy Spirit, applying the fruits of the finished work of Christ through a church constantly awakened through prayer, can deliver the lost from the power of Satan (Acts 26:17-18), as "the Lord adds daily those who are being saved" (Acts 4:47).

The awakening of the church is thus essential to the completion of world evangelization. The renewed church in Acts 2:42-47 was strengthened by apostolic teaching, by the Lord's Supper and by sharing fellowship. But these means of grace can only be empowered for us today through fervent and persistent prayer to the Father in the name of the crucified and risen Christ. Even after Pentecost, the apostles repeatedly returned to prayer for the church to be filled afresh with the Spirit and empowered to proclaim the Gospel with boldness, despite satanic resistance (Acts 4:23-31).

Prayer is God's appointed means through which the Spirit's power is released in evangelism. By prayer, the Spirit both empowers our witness and opens the blinded minds of unbelievers to seek and desire the Lord Jesus Christ as Savior. Our strong encouragement in believing prayer is our Lord's promise that He will answer us if we ask according to His will and in His name.

Before the Lord's return to judge all satanic rebellion and to consummate His Kingdom in power and glory, the Gospel must and will be preached, and disciples made, among every people on earth (Matt. 24:14; 28:19,20; Mark 13:10). Explicit agreement and visible union of God's people in extraordinary prayer for the awakening of the church and world evangelization is essential for the extension of the Kingdom of Christ through the preaching of the Gospel.

Call to Prayer

We rejoice that in the last few years, in many parts of the world, the Holy Spirit has instilled a growing dependence on God, leading to increased unity in prayer within the Body of Christ, transcending denominational, national, ethnic and cultural divisions.

We confess that too often prayer is offered only for personal physical and financial needs, rather than for spiritual and material needs in the church, neighborhood and world.

We confess that frequently there is a lack of meaningful prayer by the congregation in services of the local church, as well as a general lack of personal and family prayer.

We confess that there is not enough emphasis on, training for, and dependence upon prayer from the pulpits, and in institutions training Christian workers.

We confess that too often dependence upon the Holy Spirit's role in prayer has been minimized, and mobilization of prayer has been without reliance upon Him.

We are constrained to call the Body of Christ worldwide to mobilize intercession for spiritual awakening in the church and world evangelization. We call specifically for:

1. The formation of interdenominational prayer committees, whenever possible through existing structures, on city, national, regional, continental and international levels.
2. The convening of national, regional, continental and international prayer assemblies as soon as this can adequately be implemented, and thereafter at regular intervals.

3. The establishing of information networks through personal visitation, literature, computer linkages, audio-visual media, and other means for the communication of prayer needs, emergencies, methods, reports of prayer movements worldwide, and prayer ministry resources.
4. The promotion of nurture and teaching on prayer life through seminars, workshops, literature and audio-visuals.
5. The encouragement of churches, theological seminaries, Christian institutions, para-church organizations, Christian leaders and pastors to give the highest priority and strongest emphasis to prayer, both in personal life and ministry.
6. Cooperation and participation of the church worldwide in the observance of specifically designated days of prayer.

We therefore call all believers to a specific and personal commitment to become prayer warriors for spiritual awakening and world evangelization.

For further information on the Lausanne Committee's Intercession Advisory Group or the International Prayer Assembly follow-up, contact the:

National Prayer Committee
Concert of Prayer Project
233 Langdon Street
Madison, WI 53703

NOTES

Introduction

1. J. Edwin Orr, *The Eager Feet: Evangelical Awakenings 1790-1830*, (Chicago: Moody Press, 1975), p. 95. Used by permission.

Chapter 1

1. Lewis B. Smedes, "Preaching to Ordinary People" *Leadership*, (Fall, 1983), p. 115.
2. Ibid., p. 116 (italics added).
3. John Naisbitt, *Megatrends: Ten New Directions Transforming Our Lives*, (New York: Warner Books, Inc., 1982), p. 252. Used by permission.

Chapter 2

1. O. Hallesby, *Prayer*, (Minneapolis: Augsburg Publishing House, 1975), p. 159.
2. Lausanne Committee for World Evangelization, *Evangelism and Social Responsibility*, Occasional Paper #21, 1981, p. 49.
3. George Peters, *Evangelical Missions Tomorrow*, (Pasadena, CA: William Carey Library Publications, 1977), p. 150-151 (italics added).
4. William Bright, "Interview" *Worldwide Challenge*, January, 1983, p. 8. Used by permission. Copyright Campus Crusade for Christ, Inc.

Chapter 4

1. R.J. Lucas, *Fullness and Freedom*, (Downers Grove, IL: Inter-Varsity Press, 1983), p. 107. Used by permission.

Chapter 5
1. Richard Halverson, "On the Threshold of Something Wonderful" *Eternity*, (March, 1984), p. 24-26.
2. Kenneth Kantzer, "Reflections: Five Years of Change" *Christianity Today*, (November 26, 1982), p. 13.
3. John White, *Flirting with the World: A Challenge to Loyalty*, (Wheaton, IL: Harold Shaw Publications, 1982), p. 142.
4. A.W. Tozer, *The Pursuit of God*, (Camp Hill, PA: Christian Publications, Inc., n.d.), p. 8. Used by permission.

Chapter 7
1. John C. Miller, *Repentance and the Twentieth Century Man*, (Ft. Washington, PA: Christian Literature Crusade, Inc., 1980), p. 52.

Chapter 8
1. For more help with this and all facets of prayer mobilization, contact the National Prayer Committee, Concert of Prayer Project, 233 Langdon St., Madison, Wisconsin, 53703. They have a wealth of personnel and resources on which to draw.

Chapter 9
   Another format that could be just as effective, though quite different from that given in this chapter, goes like this: Divide the two hours into equal segments of thirty minutes each. At the beginning of each half-hour segment someone presents a ten-minute exhortation on a general issue the steering committee feels must be addressed in that particular concert. After the ten-minute exhortation, the group proceeds to pray during the remaining twenty minutes. Then the next exhortation is given, and another twenty minutes of prayer follows, and so on throughout the two-hour period. Be sure to keep the exhortations biblically based and clear on the current situation. If your steering committee feels comfortable in giving leadership in this way, I strongly urge you to try it.

Chapter 11
1. J. Oswald Sanders, *Prayer Power Unlimited* (Chicago: Moody Press, 1977), p. 107. Used by permission.